the irish

the irish gourmet

Traditional Fare and Gourmet Dishes
from Ireland's Best Hotels, Restaurants
and Pubs

Connie O'Mahoney

First published 1987 by Quinlan Press,
131 Beverly Street, Boston, MA 02114, USA

This revised UK edition 1988

British Library Cataloguing in Publication Data

O'Mahoney, Connie
  The Irish gourmet
I. Food: Irish dishes — Recipes
I. Title
641.59415.

ISBN 1 85336 063 5

*Equation is an imprint of the Thorsons Publishing Group,
Wellingborough, Northamptonshire, NN8 2RQ, England*

Printed in Great Britain by
Woolnough Bookbinding, Irthlingborough, Northamptonshire

10 9 8 7 6 5 4 3 2 1

To my grandmother, Mary Ann Mahoney, who makes the best Irish tomato juice this side of county Cork, and to my aunt, Henrietta Hundertmark Laeng, who makes the best semi-Irish potato salad in the world.

I would like to thank the Northern Irish Tourist Board, the Shannon Development Corporation and the Irish Tourist Board for their help and for providing me with photographs. Gill and Macmillan kindly gave me permission to use recipes from the *Ballymaloe Cookbook*. Most of all I want to thank all those associated with the inns, pubs, restaurants, guesthouses, country houses and castles who took the time to respond to my queries and made this book possible.

Notes to the recipes

Temperature conversions

Gas	Centigrade	Fahrenheit
¼	110	225
½	130	250
1	140	275
2	150	300
3	170	325
4	180	350
5	190	375
6	200	400
7	220	425
8	230	450
9	240	475

1 US pint = 16 fl oz (1 Imperial pint = 20 fl oz)
1 US quart = 32 fl oz
1 US cup — 8 fl oz (1 Imperial cup = 10 fl oz)
To measure an American cupful, fill to 8 fl oz on a measuring jug.

contents

introduction

May the roof above us never fall in, and may we friends gathered below never fall out. This traditional Irish toast could well be the motto of the pubs, restaurants and hotels who have contributed the outstanding recipes contained in this book. In my travels through Ireland I never fail to be impressed by the combination of charm, hospitality, superb culinary imagination and, yes, blarney that restaurants use to give their guests the utmost in atmosphere and good food.

Irish cuisine has gone unrecognized in the world of gourmet dining for too long, but as this collection attests, the epicurean dining experience is alive and thriving in Ireland, a country unrivalled for its exquisite seafood dishes and hearty traditional foods. Contemporary Irish chefs combine the best in European training with a solid traditional background. As these recipes illustrate, modern Irish cuisine excels at presenting old staples like potatoes and Guinness and shellfish in exciting new contexts.

But also included here are foods that the Irish have been eating for centuries, recipes like those for soda bread and Irish stew that have stood the test of time and appeared on countless Irish tables. Gourmet and traditional, the Gaelic eating experience is now one that you can create in your own kitchen. Welcome to a celebration of festive foods as Irish as the shamrock and as delicious as the best dishes of France and Italy. As the Irish say before eating and drinking, *slainte!*

traditional fare

Northern Irish Tourist Board

Kate Kearney's Cottage
Killarney
County Kerry

K ate Kearney's Cottage is located near the Gap of Dunloe, one of the most celebrated and impressive areas in Ireland. A wild, rugged four-mile pass through towering summits and precariously perched boulders, the Gap offers the avid hiker an exhilarating view of the beautiful Killarney lakes and the majestic Macgillycuddy Reeks. There is no better way to complete a walk through these vistas than to drop in on Kate, who serves traditional foods with an expertise developed over years.

Tel: (064) 44146
Open: All year round
Prices: Lunch £2 (12-9pm)

Spiced Apple Tart

Pastry
6 ounces flour
3 ounces butter
½ teaspoon baking powder
1 teaspoon sugar
1 teaspoon cinnamon
Pinch of salt
Yolk of egg with sufficient water
  to bind

Filling
1½ lbs. apples or 1 lb. apples
and ½ lb. prunes
½ ounce butter
A little water
1 teaspoon cinnamon
2 ounces sugar
1 standard 8″ pie plate

Slice the apples. Stew prunes, if used. Mix together apples (and prunes), cinnamon and sugar. Sift flour, salt and baking powder. Rub in the butter. Add the cinnamon and sugar. Mix with yolk of egg and water. Knead the pastry and cut off ⅓ for the lid. Roll out the larger piece of pastry, turn it and place in greased pie plate.

Put the fruit mixture into the pastry case. Roll out the remaining third of pastry and cover the tart, pressing the edges well together. Make a small hole in the lid to allow the steam to escape. Place in a hot oven, 400 degrees, for 5 to 10 minutes. Reduce heat and allow the tart to cook more slowly until the pastry is quite crisp, 35 to 45 minutes. Serve hot or cold. Sprinkle the top with sugar mixed with cinnamon.

Irish Coffee

1 jigger Irish whiskey
3 cubes sugar
1 cup coffee
Whipped cream

Gradually heat a stemmed goblet. Pour in one jigger (1⅓ ounces) of Irish whiskey. Do not substitute other whiskey. Add three cubes of sugar. Fill goblet with strong black coffee to within one inch of the brim. Stir to dissolve sugar. Top off to brim with whipped cream, slightly aerated so that the cream floats on top. Do not stir after adding cream, as the true flavour is obtained by drinking the hot coffee and Irish whiskey through the chilled cream.

Barm Brack

Barm Brack is a traditional bread eaten all year round, but particularly at Hallowe'en, when a gold ring is baked in it. Whoever gets the ring will be married within a year.

1 lb. flour
2½ cups warm milk
1 lb. raisins
4 ounces currants
2 ounces mixed chopped candied peel
3 ounces sugar
¾ ounce yeast
2 ounces butter
½ level teaspoon ground cinnamon
¼ level teaspoon nutmeg
1 egg
½ level teaspoon salt

Sieve the flour, spices and salt together and rub in the butter. Cream the yeast with one teaspoon of the sugar and one teaspoon of milk. Add the rest of the sugar to the flour mixture and blend well. Pour the warm milk and the beaten egg onto the yeast mixture and combine with the flour, etc. Beat well. Fold in the fruit, chopped peel and the ring, then cover with a cloth and leave in a warm place until the dough is twice as big. Turn out and halve. Place the mixture into two 7″ cake pans. Cover again and leave to rise for about 30 minutes. Bake in a moderate to hot oven, 400 degrees, for about 1 hour. Test with a skewer before removing from oven. Glaze the top with syrup made from one tablespoon of sugar dissolved in two tablespoons of boiling water and return to a hot oven for about 3 minutes. Cool on a wire rack.

The Corner House
Schull
County Cork

Farmers, fishermen and other locals go to The Corner House for rollicking singalongs, excellent Guinness and good food. Owner Thomas Lewman oversees the place, and he can frequently be heard praising the house's specialties in verse, as in the following rhyme:

> *Did you ever eat Colcannon*
> *That's made from thickened cream,*
> *With greens and scallions blended*
> *Like a picture in your dream?*
>
> *Did you ever take potato cake*
> *When you went off to school*
> *Tucked beneath your jacket*
> *With your book and slate and rule?*

Tel: (028) 28223
Open: All year round

Colcannon

1 lb. cooked potatoes
½ lb. cooked cabbage
4 scallions, with stems
2 tablespoons cream
2 ounces butter
Salt and pepper

Chop cooked cabbage finely. Chop scallions and cook gently in butter until soft. Drain the potatoes, season with salt and pepper and mash well. Add cooked scallions and cream. Blend potatoes into cooked cabbage, beating well over low flame. Serve hot. Serves six.

Potato Cakes

½ lb. cooked potatoes
½ teaspoon salt
½ ounce butter or margarine
2 ounces flour
¼ teaspoon baking powder
A little milk

Sift flour, salt and baking powder into a bowl. Add sieved potatoes and melted butter. Mix to a smooth dough, adding a little milk if necessary. Turn onto a floured board, knead until smooth. Divide in two. Roll out each piece to a circle ¼ inch in thickness. Cut into 6 or 8 triangles. Heat and grease frying pan or griddle. Fry cakes until nicely browned on both sides.

Corned Beef and Cabbage

4 lbs. corned beef
1 large sliced carrot
2 large onions, one stuck with whole cloves
1 large cabbage
1 teaspoon dry mustard
Parsley sprigs
Pepper
Cold water

Place the corned beef into a large saucepan with all the ingredients except the cabbage. Cover with cold water and bring to a rapid boil. Skim. Cover and simmer very gently for 45 minutes. Trim cabbage and cut into quarters. Leave a little of the stump on, as this adds flavour. Add to pot. Cook the meat for 30 minutes to the pound and serve surrounded with cabbage. Serves six.

Nettle Soup

1 leek
¼ lb. butter
1 bunch young nettles
1 lb. potatoes
5 cups chicken stock
½ cup cream
Salt and pepper

Soak the chopped leeks in the butter, add the washed and chopped nettles and cook them until they appear glossy. Stir in the peeled and sliced potatoes and add the stock. Simmer for 30 to 35 minutes. Liquidize the soup in a food processor. Return to heat. Add cream, salt and pepper. Serve hot. Serves six.

Aillwee Cave Restaurant
Ballyvaughan
County Clare

The Aillwee Cave in Ballyvaughan, with its great caverns, eerie stalactites and subterranean rivers, has been a major tourist attraction in the Burren since its discovery by a herdsman in 1976. A hibernation home for bears for thousands of years before its discovery, this beautiful natural wonder has many marvellous nooks and chambers to explore. One of over three hundred caves for which the Burren is famous, the Aillwee is one of the few that are accessible to the average tourist. After a day of spelunking, the Aillwee Cave Restaurant, with its hearty traditional recipes and excellent desserts, is a welcome sight to the hungry explorer.

Tel: (065) 77036/77067
Open: All year round (10-7pm)
Prices: Lunch up to £7.50

Aillwee Quiche

Short Crust Pastry
2 ounces shortening
4 ounces margarine
½ lb. flour
1 egg

Filling
5 eggs
¼ lb. ham
¼ lb. cheese
1¼ cup milk
½ green pepper
1 onion
Salt and pepper to taste

Rub shortening and margarine into flour lightly until mixture resembles fine bread crumbs. Add lightly beaten egg, sufficient to form a dough. Roll out and line pie plate. Blend all filling ingredients lightly together in blender and pour into prepared pan. Place in oven, 400 degrees, for 45 minutes or until golden brown and set. Serves eight.

Guinness Stew

2 lbs. lean stewing beef
1 tablespoon flour
2 tablespoons oil
2 large onions, sliced
2 large carrots, sliced
2 cups beef stock
1¼ cup Guinness stout
1 tablespoon chopped parsley
Salt and pepper to taste

Chop meat into bite-size pieces and toss in seasoned flour. Brown in a heavy pan with oil. Remove from pan and place in oven casserole with onions, carrots, stock and half the Guinness. Simmer gently for 2 hours until tender. Add remaining Guinness and chopped parsley. Check for seasoning and serve with boiled potatoes and a green vegetable. Serves four.

The Bohemian Girl
Wexford
County Wexford

In 1977 Seamus and Kay McMenamin took an old, run-down building and transformed it into their dream restaurant. Though never formally trained, Kay does all the cooking, and people swear she is the best around because she never learned how to take the short cuts. Her cooking has been good enough to win major food awards year after year. The Bohemian Girl is named after the opera of the same name by the Irish composer William Michael Balfe, who taught music and singing in this very building. The creative genius that inspired Balfe seems also to have inspired Kay.

Tel: (053) 24419
Open: All year round
Prices: Dinner £13.95 (6.30-10pm) Lunch £3 (12.20-3pm)

Cream of Celery Soup

3 ounces clarified butter
1 large onion, finely chopped
5 cups milk
1 teaspoon dried mixed herbs
3 or 4 bay leaves
10 black peppercorns
2 tablespoons plain flour
2½ cups stock
1 teaspoon salt
½ teaspoon white ground pepper

In a medium saucepan melt half of the butter. Add the onion and celery and simmer very gently for about 25 minutes or until the vegetables are soft. While the celery and onions are cooking, bring the milk, bay leaves, mixed herbs and peppercorns to the boil in a small saucepan over gentle heat. Cover the pan and simmer for about 5 minutes to extract the full flavour of the herbs, etc. Strain into a bowl and allow to cool. In a large saucepan melt the rest of the butter. Remove from the heat and add the flour and salt to make a roux. Return mix to the heat and slowly add the infused milk. Bring to a boil. Add the stock. Liquidize the celery, onion and the rest of ingredients, making sure that the roux is completely smooth. Serves six.

Wexford Mussel Chowder

6 dozen fresh mussels
4 tablespoons butter
1 large onion, finely chopped
1 tablespoon chopped parsley
1 large bay leaf
1 teaspoon of pepper
1¼ cup cider
1 leek, finely sliced
1 stalk celery, finely chopped
3 tablespoons flour
3 quarts fish stock
1 quart milk, scalded
5 ounces heavy cream

Remove beards from mussels. Discard any that are open. Put mussels in a basin and leave cold tap running gently on the basin. This gets rid of all of the sand from the mussels. Using a spoonful of butter, grease a large saucepan. Add the chopped onions, parsley and bay leaf. Put the mussels on top and season with pepper. Pour in the cider. Bring to a boil. Cover and cook for 6 to 7 minutes, shaking the pan occasionally. Remove from the heat. Take out the mussels, discarding any that haven't opened. Remove mussels from the shells and set aside. Discard the shells. In another large saucepan melt the rest of the butter over gentle heat. Add the leek and the celery and cook for about 6 minutes, stirring frequently. Remove from heat and stir in the flour. Return to heat and cook for 2 to 3 minutes. Gradually add fish stock and milk, stirring constantly. Increase the heat to moderate and bring to a boil, stirring all the time. Reduce the heat to low and simmer gently for 15 minutes. Remove from heat and stir in the reserved mussel stock. Season to taste. Add the mussel meat and bring back to a boil. Serve immediately with fresh cream garnished with a sprig of parsley. Serves four.

The Old Stand
Exchequer Street
Dublin

Dublin office workers, shop clerks and people in high finance shake off their workday worries when they step into the relaxed atmosphere of The Old Stand after a busy day. The pub also does a roaring trade at lunchtime, when patrons enjoy traditional food as they chat about horse racing, rugby, golf and Gaelic football. Sports fans and business people agree that the fare at The Old Stand is hearty and satisfying.

Tel: (0001) 770821
Open: All year round — licensing hours
Prices: Dinner £4-7 Lunch £3-5

Boiled Bacon and Cabbage

3 lb. bacon
1 medium-sized trimmed cabbage
5 large potatoes
Parsley

Place bacon in saucepan, cover with cold water and bring to a rapid boil. Skim as necessary and simmer for 1½ to 2 hours. About 40 minutes before the bacon is cooked, halve the cabbage and place alongside bacon in saucepan. Slice pototoes and add to pot. Bring back to boil, cover and let simmer until cooked. Remove the cabbage and potatoes and drain thoroughly. Garnish with parsley. Serves ten.

Coddle Dublin Style

8 thick slices bacon
1 lb. pork sausages
4 large sliced onions
8 large potatoes, peeled and
  sliced
5 cups water
Chopped parsley
Salt and pepper

Boil the sausages and bacon for 5 minutes. Remove, keeping the liquid. Put all the ingredients in an ovenproof dish, seasoning to taste. Add enough stock to cover. Cover with lid and simmer gently, or cook in a moderate oven, 225 degrees, for about 1 hour or until the ingredients form a semi-thick stew. Serves eight.

Dublin Bay Prawn Cocktail

¾ lb. cooked, shelled prawns
½ pint mayonnaise
2 tablespoons tomato paste
Dash of tabasco or Worcestershire sauce
Salt and pepper
2 drops lemon juice
1 tablespoon sherry
2 tablespoons heavy cream,
  partially whipped

Blend all the ingredients except prawns into the mayonnaise. Season to taste with salt and pepper. Arrange the shredded lettuce in the base of six individual glasses or dishes. Add the prawns. Spoon the sauce over the prawns. Garnish with lemon wedges and chopped parsley. Serves six.

Dun Aonghasa Restaurant
Kilronan
Aran Islands
County Galway

The Dun Aonghasa Restaurant high above Killeaney Bay has one of the most impressive views in Ireland. From the dining room you can see the Cliffs of Moher, the picturesque village of Kilronan and a half dozen other small towns. There is also a clear view of bustling Kilronan Harbour, with passenger ferries and fishing boats coming in and out all day long. These fishing boats bring the house speciality, fresh fish, to the restaurant. Although the Dun Aonghasa was a hill fort during more turbulent times in Irish history, today it is the site of only the best in Aran hospitality and food.

Tel: (099) 61104
Open: All year round

Cod Provençale

1 fillet of cod, skinned
2 ounces oil
1 clove garlic
½ lb. tomatoes
2 ounces dry white wine
5 ounces tomato sauce
Salt and pepper to taste
1 tablespoon chopped parsley

Coat cod in flour and fry in oil until golden brown and drain. Sweat off garlic in hot oil. Add tomatoes and cook 5 minutes. Add white wine and reduce by one half. Add tomato sauce and bring to boil. Season to taste. Add chopped parsley. Coat the fish, which has been kept hot, with the sauce and serve on a bed of rice. Serves two.

Homemade Irish Vegetable Soup

2 carrots
1 parsnip
3 stalks celery
1 leek
1 turnip
1 small head of white cabbage
1 large potato
1 medium onion
2 tablespoons cooking oil
  or margarine
1 tablespoon flour
2 quarts marrowbone stock
Hint of basil
1 tablespoon chopped parsley
Salt and pepper to taste
2 tablespoons cream

Dice all vegetables very small. Fry off in oil or margarine. Add flour. Stir into stock and bring to a boil. Simmer for 30 minutes. Add basil, parsley, salt and pepper. Serve with cream on top. Serves six.

Mussels Marinière

1 finely chopped onion
2 tablespoons chopped parsley
1 glass dry white wine
5 cups mussels
¼ cup butter and flour,
  mixed (buerre marie)
Salt and pepper to taste
Juice of ¼ lemon

Add onion, 1 tablespoon parsley and wine to the mussels. Simmer for 5 minutes. Drain, reserving stock. Keep warm. Add fish stock to liquid. Bring to a boil and whisk in buerre marie. Correct seasoning and add remaining parsley. Pour over mussels. Add lemon juice and serve. Serves four.

The Olde Railway Hotel
Westport
County Mayo

'One of the prettiest, comfortablest inns in Ireland, in the best part of town.' So English novelist William Makepeace Thackery described The Olde Railway Hotel in 1862, a description that is just as apt today. Originally a coach inn established in 1780, the hotel was a stopping-off point for travellers touring the Irish countryside by horse-drawn carriage. Horses and carts used to clop into a coachhouse at the rear of the hotel, and that coachhouse remains the same as it did 200 years ago, giving the inn a marvellous antique atmosphere.

Tel: (098) 25166
Open: January-September
Prices: Dinner £10 (6.30-9.30pm) Lunch £4 (12.30-2pm)

Gaelic Broth

1 lb. potatoes
1 lb. carrots
1 lb. onions
1 ounce dripping or butter
1 ounce cornstarch
2 ounces red lentils
2 ounces pearl barley
1 teaspoon mixed herbs
Salt and pepper to taste
10 cups meat stock
  (lamb preferably)
5 tablespoons cream
¼ cup fresh parsley, chopped

Chop all vegetables into small cubes and braise them with one ounce of dripping or butter. Add one ounce cornstarch and pour in the stock. Add lentils, barley and seasoning. Simmer for 45 minutes. Serve topped with a blob of cream and a sprinkle of parsley. If the soup turns out a little thick simply add more stock. The soup is delicious served with Irish soda bread. It is also great for keeping out the winter chill. Serves twelve.

Braised Beef in Guinness

2 lbs. lean beef
3 cups meat stock
5 ounces Guinness stout
Salt and paprika to taste
¾ lb. chopped onions
2 ounces finely ground
   breadcrumbs

Chop the meat into medium-sized cubes. Put into a saucepan and add the stock and the Guinness, salt and paprika. Bring to a boil. Then reduce heat to simmer. Chop onions and fry until golden brown. Add to the meat and leave simmer for 1½ hours over low heat. Add the breadcrumbs and let simmer for another 15 minutes. If still not thick enough the juices may be thickened with a roux. Braised Beef in Guinness can be served with homemade noodles or fresh vegetables and potato cakes. Serves six.

Homemade Noodles

1 lb. flour
1 ounce cooking oil
4 eggs
1 ounce fat
1 ounce breadcrumbs
Salt and pepper to taste

Put flour into a bowl. Add oil, eggs, pepper and salt. Knead mixture to a soft dough. Roll out very thin and let dry for an hour. Flour well and then roll like a Swiss roll. Cut into very thin strips. Put into boiling salted water and boil for 20 minutes. Strain and run under cold tap. Leave to dry. Put fat into a skillet. When hot add some breadcrumbs into the pan and then add the noodles. When golden brown on one side, using a plate, turn over to the other side and fry until golden brown. Serve immediately. Complements any meat casserole dish but especially Braised Beef in Guinness. Serves six.

Killoran's Traditional Restaurant
Hotel and Lounge
Tubbercurry
County Sligo

Killoran's is a traditional restaurant that features good home cooking and authentic Irish entertainment. This restaurant is the type tourists search for, a place of genuine tradition that treats its guests with courtesy, quality service and terrific food. Family-owned and operated, Killoran's motto is: *The welcome doesn't die on the doormat*. Antique butterchurns decorate the restaurant. Anne and Tommie Killoran deliver their personal service while maintaining a traditional theme. Good food is their point of honour.

Tel: (071) 85111
Open: All year round
Prices: Dinner £10 (6-9pm) Lunch £4 (12.30-2.30pm)

Baked Irish Stew

1 lb. mutton
1 cup raw potatoes, sliced
1 onion, chopped
1 pint of stock or cold water
1 cup clarified dripping

Wash mutton well and dry in a cloth. Cut into small pieces. Put a layer on the bottom of a pie dish. Then add a layer of sliced raw potatoes and a little pepper and salt. Add a layer of onion and a layer of meat and so on until the dish is full. Then pour over half a pint of light stock or cold water. Cover with a crush made of clarified dripping or half lard, half butter. Put into an oven at 350 degrees for 1 hour.

Fresh Mayo Salmon

1 lb. salmon
½ cup flour
1 tablespoon oil
¼ cup fresh parsley

Pan fry salmon with seasoned flour. Shake off excess. Place on a greased baking sheet or grill. Brush with oil. Grill on both sides, brushing frequently with oil, for approximately 10 minutes. Remove the centre bone. Garnish with sliced cucumber and parsley and a suitable sauce. Serves two.

Boxty

6 large potatoes
1 onion, chopped fine
2 teaspoons salt
8 ounces flour
1 teaspoon baking powder

Grate the potatoes fine. Strain the water from same. Add chopped onion, salt and flour, as well as baking powder. Mix well to a nice soft mixture. Have a greased, hot pan ready. Spread mixture thinly and cook for 5 minutes. When cooked serve hot with butter. Serves four.

Boiled Fruit Cake

8 ounces stock
8 ounces brown sugar
5 cups water
4 ounces mixed cut fruit peel
1 lb. plain flour
Half level teaspoon baking soda
1 rounded teaspoon mixed spice,
  including nutmeg
2 eggs

Place the stock, sugar and water in a saucepan and bring to a boil, stirring until the sugar is dissolved and stock has melted. Add mixed peel and simmer over a low heat for 3 to 5 minutes. Remove from heat and allow to cool until luke-warm. To speed up this mixture empty into a clean tray and stir from time to time. Sieve the flour, baking soda and spices into a large mixing bowl and make a well in the centre. Beat the eggs in small bowl and add with the cooked fruit. Stir quickly together, mixing well, and turn into the prepared pan. Bake in a preheated oven for 1½ to 2 hours at 400 degrees, 45 minutes. Serves six.

Homemade Ginger Cake

¾ cup butter
2 cups sugar
4 eggs
2 cups flour
1½ teaspoons baking powder
1 cup milk
1 teaspoon essence of ginger

Beat the butter and sugar to a light cream. Add the eggs, one at a time, beating 3 minutes after each. Sift the flour and baking powder together. Mix lightly with the butter and add the milk and essence and beat well. Have ready a well-greased cake tin. Put in the mixture and bake about 40 minutes at 400 degrees.

The Vineyard Bar
Cork City
County Cork

The Vineyard Bar on St. Patrick's Street in Cork is one of the best known sporting pubs in all Ireland. Cork has always been well known for its athletic prowess, and many of Ireland's most famous hurlers and footballers have enjoyed many a meal and drink at the 'Vin.' The previous owner, a medal winner in hurling and Gaelic football himself, purchased the 200 year-old pub in 1912, and his son has maintained the pub's sporting reputation. Players and fans of all ages bring their healthy appetites here regularly, and they are rewarded with solid traditional fare.

Tel: (021) 274793
Open: All year round
Prices: Dinner £10 (6-9pm) Lunch £4 (12.30-2.30pm)

The 'Vin' Casserole of Pork

6 shoulder pork chops
4 medium-sized sour apples
3 medium-sized onions
1½ tablespoons brown sugar
1 tablespoon cold water
Salt and pepper

Trim excess fat from pork chops and cut fat into thin strips. Peel and slice apples, then mash them. Peel and slice onions. Grease a casserole dish. Place half the mashed apples in the casserole. Cover with half the onion slices. Sprinkle this with half the sugar. Lay the pork chops side by side on top. Season with salt and pepper. Sprinkle the contents with water. Cover the chops with the remaining onion and apple. Toss the strips of pork fat in the remaining sugar. Arrange them crisscross on top of the apple and onion slices. Season again with salt and pepper. Cover tightly. Bake on middle shelf of a moderate oven, 350 degrees, for approximately 1 hour. Lower temperature to 300 degrees and cook for at least another hour. Serve with fluffy mashed potatoes. Serves six.

Seanachie
Dungarvan
County Waterford

The Seanachie Public House Restaurant and Craft Shop is a late-eighteenth-century thatched building, refurbished in 1977 with traditional fittings. The bar itself dates from 1846, and the original signpost still hangs above it. Awarding the Seanachie the Pub of the Year Award in 1983, the judges said that they were particularly impressed with the pub's 'great atmosphere and the way in which the beautiful furniture has been used to good effect.' The Seanachie (Irish for *storyteller*) has won every major food award available in the country.

Tel: (058) 46305
Open: All year round

Baked Salmon

Salmon, portioned to amount
  required per person
¼ teaspoon salt
¼ teaspoon cayenne pepper
1 teaspoon lemon juice
8 ounces cream

Take one side of salmon and cut off to the bone. Portion the salmon to size required. Take one ovenproof dish. Lay portions of salmon side by side. Season with salt and cayenne pepper and a little lemon juice. Pour cream over mixture. Bake at 350 degrees for 20 to 25 minutes or until cooked. No cover is needed on the dish. No fat other than cream. Serve with steamed buttered potatoes and baked tomatoes. Serves six.

Lamb Stew

1½ lbs. neck or shoulder
of lamb or mutton
1 lb. carrots
1 lb. onions
1½ lbs. potatoes
2-3 ounces cornstarch
2 tablespoons parsley
Plenty of salt and pepper

Take the meat and cut off the fat. Remove the bones carefully and cube the meat. Take a large casserole dish and lay the meat in it. Season very well. Cover well with water and bring slowly to a boil, skimming while doing so. Simmer for 1 hour. While the meat is cooking prepare the vegetables, cutting the carrots and onions to approximately the same size as the meat cubes. Peel potatoes. When meat has simmered for an hour add the carrots, onions and potatoes, along with seasoning. Return to boil, adding more liquid if required. Cook until potatoes are just done. Dissolve cornstarch in a little cold water. Add to stew with a wooden spoon, stirring gently. Bring again to a boil. Serve with chopped parsley on top. Serves six.

Bunny's Potato Soup

Bunny O'Sullivan bases this recipe on one her grandmother used eighty years ago.

4 large potatoes
1 medium onion
2½ cups milk
Salt and pepper to taste
½ ounce butter
2 tablespoons parsley

Peel potatoes and onion. Chop in large pieces. Cover with water in saucepan. Boil until soft. Put through food processor or blender. Return to saucepan with milk. Bring to a boil, season to taste. Add the butter. Serve sprinkled with chopped parsley. Serves six.

Beezie's Dining Saloon
Lough Gill
County Sligo

Beezie's is a hostelry dedicated to Beezie Gallagher, a kindly lady who devoted her life to looking after weary, hungry, thirsty travellers and to the animals she loved. It is said that swans sat in her kitchen and ate from her hand and that she once banned a visitor from her island who dared to throw a stone at a rat. Beezie always had the hearthfire going, ready to heat a kettle or dry the damp coat of a guest. A born entertainer, she regaled patrons with stories and folktales until far into the night. Though Beezie is no longer with us, her restaurant continues her tradition of warmth and welcome to this day.

Tel: (071) 43031
Open: All year round
Prices: Dinner £6-11 (6-10pm) Lunch £5 (12.30-3pm)

Mulligatawny Soup

1 apple
1 large carrot
2 onions
2 ounces cooking oil
1 ounce flour
1 tablespoon curry powder
5 cups stock or water
1 tablespoon chutney
1 ounce seedless grapes
Pinch of sugar
Little lemon juice or vinegar

(Beezie's recommends making stock by simmering lamb bones or a small lamb's head, but any stock will do.) Chop the apple and vegetables into tiny pieces. Toss in hot oil. Blend in flour and curry powder. Add the stock. Bring to a boil and cook until thickened. Add remaining ingredients and cook for 45 minutes to 1 hour. Strain and return to the pan to reheat. Taste, adjusting seasoning if necessary and add a little extra sugar or lemon juice if required. Serves four.

The Black Sheep Inn
Schull
County Cork

W est Cork is famous for its magnificent scenery, dramatic coastline and friendly people. In the heart of this beautiful country, one can find a restaurant whose food is as intriguing as its name— the Black Sheep Inn.

Tel: (028) 28203
Open: April-Summer
Prices: Dinner £12-14 (6.30-9.30pm) Lunch £5 (11-5pm)

Baked Stuffed Trout

3 ounces ham
2 ounces mushrooms
1 tablespoon chopped parsley
2 ounces breadcrumbs, fresh
Salt and pepper to taste
1 lemon
3 ounces butter
2 large trout, cleaved and
    washed
Cocktail sticks

Chop ham and mushrooms. Add the breadcrumbs, parsley, salt and pepper and bind with the juice of half the lemon and one ounce melted butter. Wash the trout and fill the body cavity with the stuffing. Sew up with cocktail sticks. Place the fish in a buttered, ovenproof dish. Add the remaining butter and lemon juice. Bake for 40 to 50 minutes at 375 degrees or longer if covered with foil. Serves four.

Irish Coffee Cake

4 ounces butter
4 ounces sugar
2 eggs
6 ounces flour
1 pint coffee
½ ounce gelatin, dissolved
1 tablespoon brown sugar
1 jigger Irish whiskey
1 pint whipped cream
Flaked chocolate or chopped
    almonds or walnuts

Beat the butter and sugar until white and creamy. Add the beaten eggs and mix together. Mix in the sifted flour. Put into an oblong baking pan and bake at 325 degrees for 50 minutes. Turn onto a wire tray and cool. Make coffee. Add gelatin, brown sugar and whiskey and pour evenly over the sponge. Allow to chill and spread the whipped cream over the sponge. Decorate with chocolate or nuts.

Nancy's
Ardara
County Donegal

The original Nancy established this traditional pub 300 years ago. A resiliant, tough-minded widow, she ran the pub to support her fatherless children. When she died, one of her daughters took over, and to date four generations of 'Nancys' have run the pub. Its reputation for fine food and drink is centuries old. Today, Margaret 'Nancy' McHugh maintains that reputation, and her pub is a favourite stop for tourists and locals alike.

Tel: (075) 41187
Open: All year round
Prices: Up to £6.50 (11-9pm)

Potato Bread

4 ounces flour
1 ounce butter
1 lb. potatoes
½ teaspoon salt

Boil the potatoes until done. Mash well with butter and salt, making sure there are no lumps. Blend in the flour and knead until it is elastic enough to roll out. Be careful not to overdo it, as this will toughen the dough. Roll out and cut into squares. Bake until brown on both sides in a hot, dry pan at 400 degrees for about 25 minutes.

Guinness Cake

8 ounces butter
8 ounces soft brown sugar
4 eggs
10 ounces flour
2 teaspoons allspice
8 ounces seedless raisins
8 ounces seedless grapes
4 ounces mixed candied peel
4 ounces chopped walnuts
12 tablespoons Guinness (or any dark beer or ale)

Cream the butter and sugar. Beat in the eggs and fold into flour and allspice. Add the fruit and nuts, mixing well. Pour in the Guinness, four tablespoons or more as necessary for soft dropping consistency. Put the mixture into a 7″ greased cake pan. Bake for 1 hour at 325 degrees. Bake for a second hour at 300 degrees. Allow cake to become cold and remove from pan. Prick the base with a skewer and spoon over the remaining Guinness. Allow to soak overnight. Wrap in aluminum foil and store for one week before serving.

O'Donoghue's Garage and Bar
Castletownbere
County Cork

At O'Donoghue's you can pull up a stool and get your car fixed while you quench your thirst and sample their fine fish dishes. Castletownbere is a major Irish fishing port, so most of the patrons at O'Donoghue's earn their living from the sea. The bar is certainly not pretentious—it caters to locals rather than tourists—but you can certainly count on fresh ingredients and excellent preparation from their kitchen. Their fish dishes have been a village favourite since 1920, and a visit to O'Donoghue's is the perfect way to round off a day in this beautiful Irish town.

Tel: (027) 70007
Open: All year round

Stuffed Fillets of Haddock

2 one-pound fillets of haddock
1 cup white bread crumbs
2 cloves crushed garlic
1 tablespoon chopped parsley
½ teaspoon chopped thyme
1 tablespoon melted butter
½ cup cream
2 cups mashed potatoes
1 egg (separated)
Salt and pepper to taste

Lay a fillet of haddock in a buttered casserole dish. Make a savoury stuffing by combining the bread crumbs, garlic, parsley, thyme, melted butter and seasonings. Place the stuffing on top of the fish and cover with a second fillet. Moisten with cream. Cover and bake in a moderate oven (350 degrees) for 15 minutes. Add the yoke and stiffly beaten white of the egg to mashed potatoes and spread over fish. Return to oven and brown. Serves four.

Dressed Whole Salmon

Whole salmon
Salt and pepper
Bay leaves
Slices of lemon and onion

Wrap salmon in cheesecloth to make it easy to remove the fish from the saucepan. Add salt and pepper, bay leaves, slices of lemon and slices of onion, all to taste, to boiling water. Lower the salmon into this. Return to boil and simmer very gently. Allow 3 minutes per pound for tailpiece or 5 minutes per pound for whole salmon. When cooked, leave salmon in water for 5 minutes to cool slightly. Lift out and allow to drain. Serves four to eight depending on size of salmon.

Sweet Soused or Potted Herrings

6 herrings
1 slice onion
Bay leaves

Marinade
1 cup vinegar
¼ cup brown sugar
1 bay leaf
1 finely chopped onion
¼ teaspoon mixed spice
¼ teaspoon dried thyme
¼ teaspoon pepper
1 tablespoon salt

Combine the marinade ingredients in a small saucepan and boil for 3 minutes. Allow to cool. Fillet the herrings. Place one slice of onion and a half bay leaf on tail end of fillet and roll up. Place rolled fillet in a casserole. Pour marinade over fish, cover and place in a moderate oven (350 degrees) for 15 minutes. (Long slow cooking may also be used.) Serve cold with green or apple and nut salad or serve hot. Allow one herring per portion. Serves six.

Northern Irish Tourist Board

Pat Cassidy's Public House
Liskaskea
County Fermanagh

Pat Cassidy is a gifted raconteur whose spellbinding stories attract people from all over Ireland to listen to his silver tongue. The time may be past when you could get poteen (Irish moonshine distilled from potatoes) in Cassidy's, but Pat still serves a variety of traditional breads and cakes that have been in his family for years. Boxty cake is a favourite among Pat's guests. Properly made, boxty cake should be slowly cooked all night long over a hearthfire. Pat also serves Irish soda bread from his aunt's own recipe. It is said of her bread that it would rise so high it would 'kick the lid off the oven.'

Tel: (03657) 21172
Open: All year round

Boxty Cake

12 potatoes, 6 boiled, 6 raw,
   grated
3 handfuls flour
½ teaspoon salt
Enough water for shaping

Mix well and shape into dumpling size. Bake for 1 hour at 150 degrees or boil for 1 hour.

Auntie's Irish Soda Bread

1 lb. white flour
1¼ cup buttermilk
½ teaspoon baking soda
½ teaspooon salt

Sift all the dry ingredients together and make a well in the center. Add enough milk to make thick dough. Mix well with a wooden spoon, bringing in the flour from the sides to the center. Add more milk if the mixture seems too stiff. Lift the mixture to a lightly floured board and knead lightly. Flatten the dough into a circle. Put on a baking sheet, scoring the top with a floured knife in the form of a cross. Bake in a moderate to hot oven (400 degrees) for about 40 minutes.

Sweeney's Hotel
Dungloe
County Donegal

Sweeney's started out as a tearoom in the mid-eighteenth century and became a hotel in the early nineteenth when John Sweeney made a good deal of money selling leather to the U.S. The hotel remained in the Sweeney family until 1982, when it was taken over by Morgan and Christina Delaney. Patrons of the hotel's fine restaurant have the bonus of being served by Sweeney's two amiable waitresses, Aggie and Betty, fixtures at the restaurant for over two decades who make the good food even more enjoyable.

Tel: (075) 21033/21376
Open: mid March-October, December-mid January
Prices: Dinner £11 (6-9pm) Lunch £3 (1-2pm)

Irish Stew

2½ lbs. lamb chops
   (or mutton or lamb pieces)
2 lbs. potatoes
¾ lb. onions
¾ lb. carrots
13 stalks celery
Salt and pepper to taste
Parsley
6 cups water or stock

Trim excess fat from the meat. Peel potatoes. Slice onions, carrots and celery. Place layer of potatoes in stew pan. Season lightly with salt and pepper. Add a layer of meat and a sprinkling of vegetables. Repeat layers finishing with potatoes. Add stock almost to cover. Cook covered over a slow heat for about 2½ hours until meat is tender. Take off excess fat. Sprinkle with parsley. Serve with mashed potatoes mixed with scallions and buttermilk. Serves four.

Talbot Hotel
Wexford
County Wexford

The Talbot Hotel in downtown Wexford is a bustling meetingplace for locals and out-of-town guests. The hotel is particularly famous for its nightly entertainment, but the menu, featuring freshly caught seafood, is equally crowd-pleasing. The proprietors are particularly proud of the dishes made with mussels grown in Wexford Harbour, the mussel capital of the world. As the annual Wexford Mussel Festival shows, they take their seafood seriously here, as do the chefs at the Talbot Hotel.

Tel: (053) 22566   Telex: 80658
Open: All year round
Prices: Dinner £12-15 (6.30-8.45pm) Lunch £4 (12.30-2.15pm)

Mussels à la Talbot

1 quart mussels, washed and debearded
6 tablespoons white wine
2 shredded carrots
4 tablespoons chopped onions
3 cloves garlic
1 bay leaf
4 glasses white wine
4 ounces roux
2½ cups cream
Salt and pepper to taste

Put scrubbed mussels into pot with six tablespoons cooking oil. Add carrot, onion, garlic and bay leaf. Cover with tight-fitting lid and place on full flame for 8 to 10 minutes. Mussels should have opened. Add wine and reboil for 3 minutes. Drain off all liquid into saucepan and add roux, making a thick sauce which can be thinned down with cream. Check sauce for seasoning. Add mussels to sauce and serve. Serves four.

Tripe and Onions

2 lbs. good pork tripe, chopped into large cubes
2 large shredded onions
Salt and pepper to taste
5 cups milk

Simmer all ingredients until tender, approximately ten minutes. Serves four.

gourmet dishes

Northern Irish Tourist Board

White's on the Green
Dublin

Helen Lucy Burke, restaurant critic for Dublin's *Sunday Tribune,* has named White's on the Green her City Restaurant of the Year for 1986. Citing the superb service and wonderful food, Burke describes White's, which opened on St. Stephen's Green in the heart of Dublin only a year ago, as one of the top restaurants in the country. Owners Peter and Alicia White have travelled the world for a decade, visiting outstanding restaurants as they learned what they needed to fulfil their dream of running a top-notch restaurant.

Tel: (0001) 751975
Open: All year round
Prices: Dinner £20-35 (7.30-10.30pm) Lunch £10 (12.30-2.30pm)

Grilled Sea Bass with Leek and Soya Butter

1 lb. fillet of sea bass
1 shallot, chopped
White or one leek, chopped
1 tablespoon olive oil
2 tablespoons dry white wine
1 cup fish stock
1 ounce butter
5 ounces cream
Salt and pepper to taste

Grill sea bass. Sauté shallots and leek in olive oil. Add white wine and fish stock. Add butter and cream. Reduce by half. Add soya sauce but do not boil. Season to taste. Serve on a plate with grilled sea bass, place on top of sauce. Serves two.

Ashford Castle
Cong
County Mayo

The only Irish hotel ever to receive the coveted Gold Plate Award from the distinguished Egon Ronay Guide of London, Ashford Castle offers its visitors accommodation and cuisine matched by few hotels in the world. The Castle of Cong, as it was originally known, dates back to 1228, when Richard de Burgo built his mansion on the shores of the haunting, beautiful Lough Corrib. The Guinness family purchased the castle in 1852 and, over the next thirty years, completely rebuilt Ashford at the staggering cost of two million pounds. The castle mantains that splendour to the present day, especially in its two dining rooms, which feature both haute and nouvelle cuisine. Manager Rory Murphy and head chef Denis Lenihan ensure the highest culinary standards, whether serving the casual guest or the president of the US.

Tel: (092) 46003/6   Telex: 53749
Open: All year round
Prices: Dinner £30 (7.30-9pm) Lunch £15 (1-2.15pm)

Ashford Castle's Filet de Truite Mayo
(Fillet of Trout with Spinach in Puff Pastry)

1 lb. brown or rainbow trout fillets (white fish may be substituted)
1 lb. halibut fillets
1 lb. mussels, cleaned
$1/8$ lb. (4 medium) oysters
¼ lb. bay scallops
¼ lb. shrimp, shelled and deveined
¼ cup whipping cream
1 tablespoon brandy
½ teaspoon salt
¼ teaspoon pepper
¼ lb. spinach, stems removed
½ lb. puff pastry
1 tablespoon minced parsley

Steam mussels in medium saucepan with 1 cup water for 3 to 4 minutes. Discard mussels that have not opened. Remove meat from mussels and place in blender with oysters, scallops and shrimp. Add cream, brandy, salt and pepper and purée until smooth. Set aside.

Blanch spinach leaves in boiling water for 30 seconds, remove and rinse in cold water, drain on paper towel.

Roll the puff pastry into a 10 × 13 inch rectangle. Lay one trout fillet in the centre of the pastry, top with ¼ cup of puréed fish mixture and one layer of spinach leaves. Repeat with the second trout fillet, fish mixture and spinach.

Follow same layering procedure using halibut, then repeat using remaining trout. Sprinkle with parsley. Fold pastry over, enclosing layers and smoothing pastry to an even thickness. Pinch seam together to seal.

Place fish pastry seam-side down on a rimmed baking sheet. Bake in a preheated 400 degree oven for 25 to 30 minutes.

Cashel House Hotel
Cashel
County Galway

The Cashel House Hotel, nestled in thirty-five acres of a secluded botanical wonderland in county Galway, has an international reputation for good food and first-rate accommodation. With open turf fires, the restaurant's atmosphere is warm and intimate, and the kitchen features fresh ingredients from its own garden and local harbours.

Tel: (095) 31001   Telex: 50812
Open: mid March-October
Prices: Dinner £19 (7-8.30pm) Lunch £5 (12.30-2.30pm)

Plaice Stuffed with Mussels

1 shallot, chopped
¼ lb. chopped mushrooms
¼ cup chopped chives
2 ounces butter
1¼ cups mussels, cooked and shelled
¼ lb. fresh white breadcrumbs
1 teaspoon lemon juice
Salt and pepper to taste
4 tablespoons fresh cream
12 fillets plaice
½ cup white wine

Sauté shallot, mushrooms and chives in the butter. Add mussels, breadcrumbs, lemon juice and the cream, enough to bind it together, and season. Place some of this mixture on a fillet of plaice. Make an incision down the middle of another fillet and place on top of the stuffed fillet. Place in an ovenproof dish and add a little white wine to the dish. Bake in a hot oven, 400 degrees, for 15 to 20 minutes. Serve with chive sauce or Hollandaise sauce. Serves six.

Chicken in Orange and Mustard Sauce

1 chicken
2 tablespoons Dijon mustard
2 tablespoons brown sugar
2½ cups orange juice
1 tablespoon butter
1¼ cup cream
Salt and pepper to taste
Parsley sprigs

Take the chicken off the bone and remove the skin. Cut into 1-inch cubes. Place in a bowl. Mix the mustard, sugar and orange juice and pour over the chicken. Cover and leave for 24 hours. Remove the chicken and cook in a hot pan in a little butter for a few minutes. Place the orange juice mixture in a pan and reduce by about half. Add the cream and cook until sauce thickens. Season with salt and pepper. Pour over the chicken. Garnish with slices of orange and sprigs of parsley. Serves six.

Fillet of Beef Wellington with Guinness Sauce

1 fillet of beef
Chicken liver paté
Salt and pepper
Rough puff pastry
Eggwash

Guinness Sauce
3 shallots
2½ cups water
1¼ cups Guinness
4 ounces butter
2 cups beef stock
2½ cups cream
¼ cup chopped chives

Trim the fillet and set in a hot pan. Season with salt and pepper. Brush with eggwash and cook at 400 degrees for 20 to 25 minutes for medium rare beef. Peel and chop half of shallots and fry in a little cooking oil until brown. Add the beef trimmings and fry until crisp. Add the water. Bring to a boil and reduce by half. Melt a little butter in a pan. Add the rest of the chopped shallots and cook for a few minutes. Turn up the heat and add the Guinness and beef stock. Reduce. Add the cream. Whisk in the rest of the butter and add the chives. Serve with sautéed mushrooms and sprigs of parsley. Serves eight to ten.

Clonmeen Guesthouse
Banteer
County Cork

Though called a guesthouse, *castle* would be more appropriate for the Clonmeen, where you are invited to dine and sleep like royalty. This 100 year-old palatial Victorian mansion offers luxury and grace, from the splendid atmosphere to the fine food. The modern, well-equipped kitchen starts its day with a breakfast buffet and continues until its guests are enjoying midnight snacks and fine German wines, imported directly from the vineyards. The library, billiard room and lounge are filled with elegant carvings, crystal chandeliers, large bay windows and antique furniture. Staying at Clonmeen Guesthouse is a traveller's delight.

Tel: (029) 56238
Open: mid May-October
Prices: Dinner £12-15 (7-9pm) Lunch £7 (2-3pm)

Baked Mushrooms

1 lb. fresh mushrooms
½ cup flour
1 beaten egg
½ cup breadcrumbs
1 tablespoon cooking oil

Wash and dry the mushrooms. Roll in the flour. Shake off excess flour, then put into beaten egg and lastly into the breadcrumbs. Fry in very warm cooking oil and serve with homemade tartar sauce. Serves four.

Smoked Salmon Noodles

1 lb. best Italian noodles
½ lb. Irish smoked salmon
1¼ cups cream
Salt and pepper to taste
1 teaspoon fresh dill
4 shallots

Put noodles into slightly salted, oiled boiling water and boil until tender. Cut the salmon into small pieces and put into cream with seasoning and dill. Leave aside for some time. Warm the salmon and put on noodles. Serve with slice of freshly cut salmon and shallots. Serves two.

Austrian Sachertorte

5 ounces sugar
6 ounces unsalted butter
2 eggs
6 ounces dark chocolate
3 ounces breadcrumbs

Cream majority of sugar with butter. Separate the eggs and add slowly to the creamed mixture with the melted chocolate. Beat egg whites with remaining sugar and fold in with the breadcrumbs. When cold decorate with chocolate and whipped cream. Bake in a preheated oven at 350 degrees for 15 minutes. Serves four.

Drimcong House Restaurant
Moycullen
County Galway

Helen Lucy Burke, food critic for Dublin's *Sunday Tribune,* has given the Drimcong House Restaurant her highest rating, proclaiming chef/proprietor Gerard Galvin an artist for his wizardry in the kitchen and awarding the Drimcong with the title of 'Country Restaurant of the Year' for 1986. The cuisine in this excellent restaurant is in the classic style, tempered continually by experiment and new ideas. Menus change weekly, influenced by what is best in the garden, in the lake outside the door and in Galway Bay. A 350 year-old estate house, Drimcong House was a private residence until the Galvins purchased it in 1984. The homey yet posh atmosphere includes Irish crystal stemware, polished oak tables and turf fires in the winter.

Tel: (091) 85115
Open: March-December (Tues to Sat)
Prices: Dinner £14.95 (7-10pm)

Drimcong Oyster Broth

2½ cups fish stock
5 ounces thin cream
12 oysters
1 teaspoon of chopped fennel or dill
1 glass dry white wine
4 drops tabasco sauce
Salt and pepper to taste

Heat the stock. Add the cream and reduce for a minute, briskly. Chop each oyster in four and add to the broth with oyster juice, wine and herbs. Season with salt and pepper and add for each portion a drop of tabasco sauce. Heat again and serve. Serves four.

Mussels and Sweetbreads in a Spinach Parcel

1 lb. lamb sweetbreads
10 cups mussels
1 glass white wine
4 spinach leaves
1 tablespoon chopped parsley
¼ lb. mushrooms
1 medium onion and one small onion
1 garlic clove
5 ounces cream
1 tablespoon chopped lemon balm

Prepare sweetbreads by boiling in a stock and simmering for 1 minute. Discard gristle and cool. Prepare mussels and open over heat in a sealed pot with white wine, small onion and parsley. Cool and shell. Steam spinach for 2 minutes and set aside. Reduce finely chopped mushrooms, onion, garlic, cream and lemon balm in an open pan until thick. Cool. Combine mussels, sweetbreads and the reduction in equal quantities. Wrap in spinach and enclose in buttered aluminum foil. Steam for 6 minutes. Peel off foil. Serve with a purée of carrots and soft cheese or by itself with lemon quarters. Serves six.

The Haven Hotel
Waterford
County Waterford

In 1850 the original house of what is now The Haven Hotel was owned by a Scottish family called Malcolmson who were in the leather, cotton and ship-building industries. Because they sided with the Confederates during the American Civil War, they lost everything, and the house passed out of their hands. Today, The Haven is a popular getaway for Irish, American and British families. The staff at the hotel is particularly attentive to children, making this historic house the ideal holiday hotel for all the family.

Tel: (051) 83150
Open: April-September
Prices: Dinner £13 Lunch £2.50

Prawns Provençale

1 large onion, chopped
1 tablespoon cooking oil or butter
1 clove garlic, chopped
½ lb. mushrooms, sliced
2 glasses chablis
2 egg yolks, beaten
2 tablespoons tomato purée
4 dozen prawns, cooked
  and peeled

Sauté onions in butter or oil with garlic. Add mushrooms and cook. Add wine and cream mixed with beaten yolks of eggs and tomato paste and cook for 10 minutes. Allow sufficient time for all ingredients to cook and thicken. Add prawns. Cook for 2 to 3 minutes. Serve with boiled rice. Serves four.

Chicken à la King

4 breasts of chicken
2 tablespoons cooking oil
    or butter
1 large onion, chopped
½ lb. mushrooms, sliced
1 clove garlic
1 red pepper, sliced
2 glasses sherry
2 egg yolks
1¼ cup cream
Salt and pepper
2 ounces cooked peas

Cook breasts of chicken in butter or oil and leave aside. To the oil add the chopped onion. Cook lightly. Add sliced mushrooms, garlic and sliced pepper. Add sherry. Beat the yolks into the cream and add to pan with the salt and pepper to taste. Add the peas. Let the mixture cook until it thickens sufficiently. Return the chicken breasts and simmer for a further 10 to 15 minutes. Serve on a bed of rice or with boiled potatoes. Serves four.

Steak Haven

4 sirloin steaks
2 tablespoons oil or butter
1 large onion, chopped
½ lb. mushrooms, sliced
1 garlic clove, crushed
1 jigger Irish whiskey
5 ounces cream
Salt and pepper to taste

Cook the steaks as required in butter or oil and set them aside. To the oil add the chopped onion. Cook lightly and add the mushrooms and crushed garlic. Add the whiskey and allow to flare for a few seconds. Beat the yolks into the cream and add to the sauce with salt and pepper to taste. Let the mixture cook very slowly for several minutes until it thickens sufficiently. Return the steaks to the sauce. Cook for a further 2 to 3 minutes. Serve steaks covered with the sauce. Serves four.

Dromoland Castle
Newmarket-on-Fergus
County Clare

Many people feel that Dromoland Castle in Newmarket-on-Fergus is one of the most beautiful castles in Ireland. Now a resort hotel, the castle retains the atmosphere of its sixteenth-century beginnings, but indulges its guests with every modern-day convenience. Reminders of the castle's past are everywhere, from the original oil paintings in the halls to the intriguing walled garden. The stately dining room and marvellous food are in keeping with this fairy-tale castle in county Clare.

Tel: (061) 71144   Telex: 70654
Open: All year round
Prices: Dinner £27 (7-9pm) Lunch £16.50 (1-2pm)

Prawn Bisque

¼ lb. butter
½ lb. diced onions, leeks, celery, carrots
2 lbs. fresh prawns, shelled (keep shells)
¼ lb. flour
10 cups good fish stock
¼ teaspoon cayenne pepper
¼ teaspoon paprika
¼ teaspoon basil
3 tablespoons tomato purée
1 jigger brandy
1¼ cups cream
Chopped parsley

Melt the butter in a large saucepan. Add mixed vegetables and prawn shells. Cover and simmer for 20 minutes. Mix in flour. Leave the mixture to cool. Pour in the hot fish stock and all the ingredients except brandy, cream and chopped prawns. Cook for another 45 minutes. Strain the soup. Before serving add the brandy, cream and prawns and sprinkle with a little chopped parsley. Serves four.

Whiskey Mousse

1 quart vanilla ice cream
1 packet lemon gelatin
2½ cups cream
1 jigger Irish whiskey

Beat the ice cream. Melt gelatin in small drop of hot water. Add cream to ice cream and pour in the gelatin and whiskey. Pour into glasses or moulds and leave to set. Serves eight to ten.

Park Hotel Kenmare
Kenmare
County Kerry

O n Easter Sunday in 1897 the elegant Park Hotel opened its doors to the public in the picturesque railway village of Kenmare. Huge four-poster beds and lavish antique furnishings still enchant guests in this exquisite castle hotel. The food here is as inspired as the decor. The superb cuisine has won nine major food awards, including Bord Failte's Award for Excellence and the Egon Ronay Hotel of the Year 1988. Head chef Matt Darcy is responsible for many original creations.

Tel: (064) 41200/41097 Telex: 13905
Open: Easter-mid November
Prices: Dinner £29 (7-8.45pm) Lunch £14 (1-2pm)

Avocado in Puff Pastry with a Fresh Tomato Sauce

1 large ripe avocado
2 ounces fresh white crabmeat
8 ounces puff pastry
1¼ lb. ripe tomatoes, skinned
 and seeded
1 ounce shallots, finely chopped
½ clove garlic, skinned and
 crushed
2 sprigs thyme and rosemary
One bouillon chicken cube
Salt and freshly ground black
 pepper
Juice of ½ lemon
1 egg white

Sauce
Remove seeds, skin and excessive juice from tomatoes. Sauté shallots and garlic in nonstick pan for 3 to 4 minutes, stirring constantly. Add herbs and sauté for 1 minute. Add tomatoes and stock, simmering for 10 to 12 minutes. Remove herbs and purée the rest in blender. Place sauté back in pan, bring to boil, skim and season to taste.

Avocado in Puff Pastry
Halve avocado, remove seed and skin. Sprinkle with lemon juice and season. Check crabmeat for shell, squeeze out excessive liquid and season to taste. Fill half avocado hollow with crabmeat. Roll out pastry to 5x4 inches, less than $1/_8$ inch thick. Place over avocado and fold under. Whisk with egg white and place on oiled tray. Place in hot oven for 5 to 7 minutes (400 degrees). Spoon sauce on plate. Place avocado on sauce, hollow side down. Serves two.

Pan Fried Veal Escalope with a Scallop Mousse and Two Sauces

4 escalopes of veal
Salt and freshly ground
  black pepper

Scallop Mousse
10 ounces fresh scallops
1½ teaspoons salt and freshly
  ground black pepper
1 whole egg and one egg white
1 pint cream
1 ounce melted butter
4 scallop corals
Squeeze of lemon juice

Spinach Sauce
4 ounces minced spinach
8 ounces double cream
Salt and black pepper
Nutmeg
½ leek, diced
½ onion, diced
2 ounces diced unsalted butter

Lobster Sauce
8 fl. ounces lobster glaze
½ onion, finely chopped
1 carrot, finely chopped
2 sprigs parsley, finely chopped
5 peppercorns
1 clove
2 tablespoons cognac
4 fl. ounces dry white wine
A little cream

Scallop Mousse
Blend all the ingredients with the exception of the four scallop corals and the cream. Remove from blender and fold in cream. Grease moulds. Place one coral in the bottom of each mould and the fill to the top with mousse mixture. Cover with buttered greaseproof paper and poach in a tray of boiling water in the oven for 8 to 10 minutes.

Spinach Sauce
Sauté leek, onion and spinach. Add seasoning, nutmeg and a little cream. Allow to cool slightly and blend. Return to pan, whisk in the butter gradually. Add the remaining cream. Adjust seasoning and serve.

Lobster Sauce
Sauté the finely chopped vegetable and parsley. Add the cognac and flame. When the flames die down add the lobster glaze. Gradually work in wine and cream. Adjust seasoning and serve.

Veal Escalopes
Season the escalopes. Place in a well-heated, heavy pan with a little oil. Seal quickly on both sides. Reduce heat and allow to cook for 8 to 10 minutes until the meat is sufficiently cooked.

To serve: Coat serving dish with the two sauces. Put remaining sauce in sauce boat. Arrange veal escalopes and mousses on the dish. Serves eight.

Ramore Restaurant
Portrush
County Antrim

The Ramore Restaurant and Wine Bar overlooking busy Portrush Harbour is a family-run establishment, with son-in-law George the inventive head chef. Father John and daughter Jane run the bar, while mother Joy oversees. The Ramore changes the menu with the seasons, creating dishes with imagination and flair. Plenty of fresh herbs are used in the flavouring and presentation of the dishes, and all the ingredients are local, including fish caught in Portrush Bay, lamb raised in nearby Ballymoney and fruit grown in neighbouring orchards.

Tel: (0265) 824313
Open: mid February-mid January
Prices: Dinner £15 Lunch £3-5

Money Bags of Seafood

1 lb. seafood of your choice
2 tablespoons sherry vinegar
4 pink peppercorns
4 large crêpes
1 medium leek, julienned

Lightly poach the fish after boning and skinning and cutting into bite-sized pieces. Allow to cool. Moisten with sherry vinegar. Add pink peppercorns. Place in the centre of the crêpe and draw up to form a little money bag. Tie with thin strips of leek (the green part). Cook in moderate oven, 350 degrees, for 10 minutes. Serve with Cream Fish Sauce. Serves four.

Quennels of Turbot in Prawns

1 lb. turbot, boned and skinned
2 egg whites
½ lb. fresh prawns, cooked and shelled
5 ounces heavy cream
Salt and pepper to taste
Dill for garnish

Make a mousseline of the turbot. Place fish and egg whites in a food processor and process for 2 minutes. Work in the cream slowly, using a spatula. Add the chopped prawns and season well. Using two spoons, form the mixture into quennel shapes and lightly poach for 5 to 10 minutes. Serve with Cream Fish Sauce and garnish with whole prawns and pieces of fresh dill. Serves four.

Cream Fish Sauce

1¼ cups fish stock
2 tablespoons dry white wine
5 ounces heavy cream
Salt and pepper to taste

Place the fish stock in pan. Reduce by ¹/₈. Add the wine and cream. Boil vigorously until thickish. Season to taste.

Ballyseede Castle Hotel
Tralee
County Kerry

O nce the chief garrison of the legendary Fitzgerald family, Ballyseede Castle was granted as a perpetual lease to Sir Edward Denny, Governor of Kerry, following the defeat of the Fitzgeralds in 1584. His rent was a single red rose presented to Queen Elizabeth on Midsummer's Day. Today, the castle maintains the elegance and majesty of the past. Amid handcarved cornices and marble fireplaces, diners at the castle restaurant enjoy a fine selection of continental and traditional Irish cuisine created by head chef Guy De Schryver.

Tel: (066) 25799
Open: All year round
Prices: Dinner £13-15 (7-9pm)

Baked Mussels Bouchon

1-2 lbs. bouchon mussels
5 ounces white wine
3-4 stalks celery
¼ cup parsley, chopped
1 onion, chopped
3 cloves garlic, chopped
½ teaspoon thyme
1 ounce butter
1 cup fresh breadcrumbs

Scrub and beard the mussels and clean them in several changes of clean water. Place them in a large saucepan with the wine and celery stalks and steam them until open. Shell and cool in their own juice. Prepare a garlic butter with parsley, onion, garlic, thyme and butter. Put the mussels in an ovenproof dish without the juice. Cover with the breadcrumbs and the garlic butter and cook in oven at 350 degrees for 15 minutes. Serves four.

Midas Veal

3½-4 lbs. boneless veal rump
  roast, rolled and tied
1 tablespoon salt
1 teaspoon fresh thyme
1 teaspoon fresh ground pepper
¼ cup vegetable oil
¼ lb. clarified butter
1 cup leeks, chopped
  (white part only)
1 cup carrots
1 cup celery
2 cups brandy
1 bottle dry white wine
½ cup cream
Salt and pepper to taste

Vegetable Garnish
1 lb. baby carrots
1 lb. small white turnips
1 lb. green beans
1 lb. small silver onions

Preheat the oven to 325 degrees. Prepare the veal. Rub the roast all over with salt, thyme and pepper. Warm the oil and butter over moderate heat and sear the roast, turning to brown all sides. Remove to a platter and cover to keep warm. Drain off all fat in casserole. Wipe out any burned residue. Add the remaining butter and warm until butter sizzles. Add leek and carrots together with celery. Place a buttered piece of waxed paper over the vegetables and cook until tender. Return the veal roast with any of the juices that have collected to the casserole. Pour the brandy over the roast and ignite. When flames subside add the white wine. Cover the casserole and place in the oven. Cook for 1½-2 hours at 350 degrees. Then remove from oven and let rest for 15 minutes.

To prepare vegetables:
Steam the carrots whole, turnips, green beans and onions separately until tender but slightly crunchy. Transfer the cooked veal to a heated platter. Skim off the fat from the liquid in the casserole. Strain the remaining pieces through a fine sieve into a medium saucepan. Add the remaining ½ cup of brandy and boil until the liquid is reduced to ⅔ of its volume. Whisk the cream. Season with salt and pepper. Serves four.

The Gresham Hotel
Dublin

One of the finest hotels in Ireland is the Gresham, located on O'Connell Street in the heart of Dublin. In existence since 1817, the hotel was destroyed during the political troubles of the 1920s, and the present building dates from 1927. Over the years the Gresham has hosted many of Europe's royal families, as well as world leaders like President Eisenhower, Italy's King Umberto and Prince Ranier and Princess Grace. Annually, 80,000 guests enjoy the hotel's ambiance, style and excellent restaurant, known throughout Europe for its fine gourmet food.

Tel: (0001) 746881   Telex: 32473
Open: All year round
Prices: Dinner £14 (6-9.30pm) Lunch £13 (12.30-2pm)

Delice of Sole Ulysses

4 folded fillets of sole
2 cups fish stock
1 glass white wine
8 prawns
¼ ounce finely diced onion
1 sliced potato
8 small mushrooms
8 slices of small cucumber
Lemon juice
1 jigger whiskey
1 ounce butter
5 ounces cream
5 ounces fish veloutê
Chervil
Flesh of one peeled tomato
Segments of one lemon

Poach the sole in fish stock and white wine. In a separate pot steam the prawns, onion, mushrooms, cucumber and potato. Add the garlic, lemon juice and butter. Flame with a glass of whiskey. Add the cream and veloutê. Remove the sole from the pot, reduce fish stock and add the sauce to it. Add the tomato. Pour the sauce into a deep dish and place the sole on top. Sprinkle with segments of lemon. Decorate with a sprig of chervil and some pieces of tomato flesh. Serves four.

Omelette Lady Caroline

3 large prawns (shelled and
   cleaned)
2 ounces clarified butter
1 teaspoon diced onion
2 small button mushrooms, sliced
¼ clove garlic
1 teaspoon peeled cucumber, cut
   in strips
1 jigger of Pernod
Juice of ¼ lemon
Pinch of chopped chervil
¼ pint cream
Flesh of 1 peeled tomato, cut in
   strips
3 eggs
Salt and pepper

Gently cook the prawns in 1 ounce of butter. Add the onion, mushroom, garlic and cucumber. Flame with Pernod. Add lemon juice and chervil. Blend in cream. Remove from heat and add tomato. Prepare folded omelette in usual fashion. Make an incision in the top and fill with garnish of prawns in sauce. Serves one.

Gaby's Seafood Restaurant
Killarney
County Kerry

With their motto of *simplicity and freshness*, Gaby's Seafood Restaurant prides itself on serving fresh, locally caught seafood in an unspoiled manner without the use of overpowering sauces and misleading, glamorous titles. Ireen and Gaby Maes combine their love of the sea with a passion for good food and wine in this charming restaurant, and their son Geert is the head chef. Gaby's is a cottage-style restaurant with plaster walls and plenty of wood. Paintings by contemporary Irish and Flemish artists grace the walls.

Tel. (064) 32519
Open: mid March-mid November
Prices: Dinner £19 (6-10pm) Lunch £10 (12.30-2.30pm)

Gaby's Creamed Potatoes

1 lb. White Rose potatoes
½ cup whipping cream
Salt and freshly ground pepper

Boil potatoes in enough water to cover until tender. Let cool. Peel. Slice ¼ inch thick. Arrange in slices in single layer (do not overlap) in four small or one large gratin dish. Whip cream to stiff peaks. Spread over potatoes. Preheat broiler. Broil as close to heat source as possible until browned, about 2 minutes. Season with salt and pepper and serve. Serves four.

Gaby's Seafood Mosaic

1 king scallop
2 ounces fresh salmon
¼ fillet of small Dover sole
   (black sole)
¼ fillet of plaice
¼ small John Dory fillet
2 ounces brill
1 oyster
1 crab claw without shell

Place plate in a very hot oven and heat until quite hot. Remove plate from oven and place lump of butter on plate. Place raw slices (wafer-thin) on butter that has melted. Decorate with lemon and parsley and serve quickly before salmon has chance to cook much. Individual portions can be made as large or small as you wish.

Lobster Gaby

1 three-pound live lobster
10 cups vegetable stock
2 ounces chopped onion
¼ lb. butter
1 ounce tomato purée
Salt and pepper
1 pinch of paprika
1 jigger Irish whiskey
1¼ cup cream

Boil lobster in vegetable stock and cool. Remove all meat from body and claws and chop into one-inch chunks. Sauté onion in butter in copper pan. Add purée, salt and pepper and whiskey and cool. Add flowing cream and thicken to preference. Empty mixture into lobster shell and place lumps of butter atop the mixture. Brown in a very hot oven. Serve piping hot. Serves two. This is the chef's secret recipe and the house specialty.

Restaurant Mirabeau
Sandycove
County Dublin

One of the finest French restaurants in Ireland, the Mirabeau is the fulfilment of a lifelong dream of owners Eoin and Doreen Clarke, who traded established careers for the pursuit of gastronomic excellence. Overseeing a staff that is entirely French, head chef Michel Flamme, who has presided over fine kitchens throughout the world, creates what the Clarkes call Cuisine Moderne, a blend of nouvelle cuisine and Irish traditional. The restaurant has its own salad and herb garden, which supplies eight varieties of lettuce and over thirty different herbs. The Clarkes claim that the only thing frozen in their kitchen is the ice cream—and even that they make themselves.

Tel: (0001) 809873
Open: All year round
Prices: Dinner £15-30 (7.30-10pm) Lunch £7 (12.30-2pm)

Pan-Fried Fillet of Beef with Meaux Mustard, Hazelnuts and Chives

1 one-pound heart of fillet of beef, cut in two
Salt and pepper
1 cup cream
2 teaspoons Meaux mustard
½ teaspoon Dijon mustard
1 ounce grilled shelled hazelnuts, finely chopped
2 ounces unsalted butter
A sprinkling of very finely chopped chives

Season the fillets with salt and pepper and pan-fry as desired. When the fillets are cooked leave them rest for 10 minutes and save the cooking juices. Add the cooking juices to deglaze the frying pan. Add cream and leave to reduce. Add the two kinds of mustard, the hazelnuts and the butter bit by bit. Adjust seasoning. Place the fillets in a very hot oven to reheat them. Just before serving sprinkle the sauce with chives. Serves two.

The Cedar Lodge Hotel and Restaurant
Newbawn
County Wexford

Located beneath the slopes of historic Carrigbyrne Forest, surrounded by the fertile fields of Slabh Coillte and the John F. Kennedy Memorial Park, the Cedar Lodge is specially tailored for people who want a relaxing holiday in pleasant surroundings. The dining room has a cedar wood ceiling, paintings by local artists and an open fire in the centre of the room. The cosy atmosphere ideally compliments the great meals prepared by owners Tom and Ailish Martin.

Tel: (051) 28386
Open: mid February-mid January
Prices: Dinner £16.50-18 (6.30-9pm)

Chicken in Cabbage Leaves

8 cabbage leaves
8 chicken breasts, skinned and
   boned
Salt and pepper to taste
16 juniper berries
4 slices of bacon
1 tablespoon melted butter

Preheat oven to 450 degrees. Remove tough stalks from cabbage leaves and boil briefly. Season chicken with salt, pepper and crushed juniper berries. Place a half slice of bacon on each and wrap in a cabbage leaf. Brush with melted butter. Place in a greased, ovenproof dish and bake for 30 minutes.

Red Mullet with Cognac

4 red mullet
2 tablespoons flour
1 tablespoon oil
4 tablespoons butter
Salt and pepper
1 glass cognac

Clean the fish and dust with flour. Fry in very hot oil and a little butter for about 10 minutes, turning once. Remove fish and keep warm. Add a generous knob of butter, plus cognac. Heat through and pour over fish. Serves four.

Fillet of Beef with Madeira and Mushroom Sauce

5 cups well-flavoured beef stock
3 fluid ounces red wine
4 tablespoons red wine vinegar
5 tablespoons Madeira
4 ounces wild mushrooms, stalks separated
Salt and pepper to taste
1 tablespoon butter
6-ounce fillet steaks

Put stock, wine, vinegar and Madeira in a large, heavy pan with the mushroom stalks. Bring to a boil and simmer until reduced to 5 ounces. Strain into a small pan and keep gently warm. Season with salt and pepper. Fry mushrooms in butter and remove. Fry steaks to your liking. Arrange mushrooms on each plate and spoon over a little sauce. Place steak on each plate and serve. Serves six.

Sea Bass with Seaweed

2 handfuls fresh seaweed
Salt and pepper to taste
1 three-pound sea bass
1 glass dry white wine

Sauce

1 tomato, seeded and finely chopped
1 sweet pepper, diced
2 tablespoons chopped herbs
Salt and pepper to taste
Juice of 2 lemons
3 tablespoons olive oil

Place ⅓ of the seaweed in a shallow, ovenproof dish. Clean and season bass. Place it on top and cover completely with remaining seaweed. Pour white wine over it. Cover dish and cook for approximately 30 minutes at 425 degrees. Combine tomato, sweet pepper and herbs and mix well. Season with salt and pepper and thin with the lemon juice and olive oil. Serve sauce separately.

Smuggler's Inn
Waterville
County Kerry

With a breathtaking, panoramic view of the sea in the scenic Ring of Kerry, the Smuggler's Inn offers its guests quality food in a charming atmosphere. It is a family-run restaurant with exceptionally fine seafood from local harbours. Winner of the Bord Failte Award, the restaurant is under the personal supervision of proprietors Lucille and Harry Hunt. Harry is also the head chef, responsible for the variety of original creations that have made the Smuggler's Inn famous.

Tel: (0667) 4330/4422
Open: May-September
Prices: Dinner £15 (6.30-10pm) Lunch £9 (12.30-3pm)

Fresh Turbot Poche Bonne Femme

5 large peeled potatoes
1 egg yolk
¼ teaspoon nutmeg
5 lbs. fresh turbot
8 ounces fresh mushrooms, sliced
2 teaspoons fresh parsley, chopped
1¼ cups dry white wine
1¼ cups heavy cream
4 ounces butter
1 tablespoon anchovy essence

Duchess Potatoes
Cook potatoes until done. Mash. Add egg and nutmeg.

Turbot
Fillet turbot into quarter-fillets. Place on ¾-inch butter tray with chopped onions and sliced mushrooms. On top of fish fillets add chopped parsley. Pour white wine over all of this. Bring to a boil and remove from heat. Pour off the stock from the turbot into a pot and allow to reduce by one half. Add the cream and allow to heat again. Then put in knobs of butter. Watch it thicken. Add the anchovy essence. Place fish on serving plates with a border of Duchess Potatoes (piped). Coat with the wine sauce and serve immediately. Serves four.

Avocado Pear and Seafood Smuggler's Style

1 whole ripe avocado
¼ lb. butter
½ small onion, finely chopped
½ clove garlic, chopped
1 diced tomato
1 teaspoon red pepper, diced
2 mushrooms, sliced
6 large jumbo scampi
1 ounce claw crab meat
10 cooked mussels
½ teaspoon of tomato paste
Cayenne pepper to taste
Salt to taste
5 ounces whipped cream
1 tablespoon of Swiss cheese
Parsley sprigs

Cut avocado in half. Remove stone. Peel off the skin. Place avocado in a gratinée dish. Put under grill at a low heat with a dab of butter with butter brush. Sauté onion, garlic, tomato pepper and mushrooms in butter over a low heat. Add seafood. Allow fish to heat thoroughly. Add tomato paste and a sprinkle of cayenne pepper and salt. Remove avocado from grill and fill with the seafood mixture. Put cream in skillet. Add Swiss cheese. Reduce and thicken. Spoon this creamy cheese sauce over the avocado halves, which have been filled with the seafood mixture. Gratinée under grill. Serve hot with a sprig of parsley on top. Serves two.

Ashbourne House Hotel
Glouthaune
County Cork

Once known as the Harmony Lodge because of the melodic sounds of the large number of wild birds nesting on the property, the Ashbourne House is a charming, cosy country-house hotel built in the early nineteenth century. Its magnificent botanical garden overlooking the River Lee features magnolia, eucalyptus, flame trees, camelia and rose beds—a kaleidoscopic bouquet for the eyes of visitors to the hotel's fine restaurant, where the food is as delightful as the scenery.

Tel: (021) 353319
Open: All year round
Prices: Dinner £15 (7-10pm) Lunch £8 (12.30-3pm)

Sautéed Prawns in Tomato and Garlic Sauce

1 small onion
2 medium-sized tomatoes
1 tablespoon cooking oil
8 ounces shelled prawns
2 cloves garlic, crushed
2½ cups cream
Salt and pepper to taste
½ ounce chopped parsley

Dice onions. Crush tomatoes. Heat oil and sauté prawns lightly with onion and crushed garlic. Add crushed tomato. Cook lightly. Add cream, seasoning and parsley. Cook until sauce thickens. Place on serving dish. Garnish with lemon wedges, lettuce, cucumber and tomato. Serves two.

Quiche Ashbourne Style

8 ounces short crust pastry
3 ounces cooked ham
2 ounces onion
2 ounces mushrooms
2 eggs
5 ounces milk
Pinch of mixed herbs
Pinch of salt and pepper
3 ounces grated Cheddar cheese
1 tomato

Grease one 8″ pie plate. Roll out pastry and line pan completely. Dice ham and onion. Slice mushrooms. Mix together and place in pan. Beat eggs and add warm milk, herbs and seasoning. Pour onto the dish. Cover with grated cheese and sliced tomato. Bake in moderate oven, 350 degrees, for 30 to 40 minutes. Serves two.

Sautéed Strips of Fillet Steak in a Cream Sauce

1 lb. fillet steak
1 medium-sized onion
4 ounces mushrooms
1 tablespoon cooking oil
½ glass white wine
5 ounces cream
Salt and pepper to taste
½ ounce chopped parsley

Cut steak into long, thin strips. Dice onion and slice mushrooms. Heat oil in a large heavy pan. Add meat, onions and mushrooms. Fry until meat is lightly cooked. Drain off excess fat. Add white wine, cream, seasoning and parsley. Allow to cook until sauce thickens. Place on serving dish and garnish with lettuce, tomato and cucumber. Serves two to three.

Baked Sea Trout With Seafood Stuffing

4 medium-sized sea trout
3 ounces sage and onion stuffing
5 ounces cooked seafood
  (prawns, salmon, cod and
  mussels)
4 ounces butter
Squeeze of lemon juice
1 ounce chopped parsley

Clean trout and remove heads. Mix together stuffing and cooked seafood which has been broken up in small pieces. Stuff the trout with the mixture. Place on a greased tray and cover each trout with a little butter. Cover with tinfoil. Cook at 325 degrees for 20 to 25 minutes. Melt butter. Add lemon juice and parsley. Put trout on serving dish and skin. Pour butter over the trout. Serves four.

Medallions of Pork Steak in Apricot Sauce

1 pork steak
1 tablespoon cooking oil
1 small onion
1 clove garlic, crushed
1 ounce flour
5 ounces brown stock
1 small can apricots with juice
1 tablespoon vinegar
1 ounce brown sugar
Salt and pepper to taste

Trim pork steak and cut into bite-sized pieces. Dice onions. Fry with pork and garlic in hot oil. Drain off excess fat. Add flour and mix well. Add stock and two tablespoons of apricot juice, four crushed apricots, vinegar, sugar and seasoning. Cook until sauce boils. Place on serving dish. Arrange rest of apricots on top and serve with savoury rice. Serves two.

Auberge de Seneirl
Bushmills
County Antrim

L ost in the countryside of Northern Ireland, close to the River Bush (famous for the Old Bushmills Distillery) is the cosy French restaurant and inn, Auberge de Seneirl. Originally an old country school, the restaurant is famous for its *table d'hôte* menus that attract clientele from as far away as the counties of the Republic. Virtually all of the dishes in this chef-owned, family-run restaurant are original creations in the tradition of high-quality French cuisine. Every ingredient is fresh; everything is made on the premises. The variety of special drinks and excellent dips make the Auberge a restaurant with a delightful change of pace.

Tel: (02657) 41536
Open: All year round
Prices: Dinner £15 (Wed to Sat)

Chicken and Fennel Terrine with Poached Pears

6 pears
2½ cups water
8 ounces sugar
1 tablespoon lemon juice
1 small chicken (2½ lbs.)
1 fennel
Salt and pepper to taste
1 clove of garlic
5 ounces cream
2 egg whites
1 lb. blueberries
A pinch of rosemary

Peel and core the pears, leaving the stock on. Bring the water and the sugar to a boil. Place the pears in the water with sugar and add the lemon juice. Cover with greaseproof paper and gently poach in a moderate oven, 350 degrees, for 20 minutes or until the pears are soft. Bone the chicken and liquidize in a food processor. Cut up the fennel. Leave a few stocks of fennel to decorate. Add to the mixture. Add seasoning, garlic and rosemary. Continue to process until a creamy mixture is obtained. Add the lightly whipped cream. Fold in the whipped egg whites. Thinly slice two of the cooked pears. Line a mould with the slices and fill in with the mixture. Poach in a bain-marie in a moderate oven, 350 degrees, for 1 hour. Allow to cool. Stew the fresh blueberries with the pear syrup. Pass through a strainer. To finish the dish, pour the sauce onto a plate, turn over the chicken and fennel terrine with a sharp knife. Decorate with a whole pear, sliced in a fan shape. Serves six.

Ballymaloe House
Midleton
County Cork

Ballymaloe House is part of an old Geraldine castle set in the middle of a 400-acre farm. A warm, comfortable home away from home for its guests, Ballymaloe features a restaurant that has won many major food awards, including the Cesar Ritz Award from Britain's Good Hotel Guide and honours from Michelin and Egon Ronay. According to the New York *Daily News*, Ballymaloe House 'is a mecca for Irish country-house cooking based on home-grown ingredients.' James Beard has praised the restaurant's 'extraordinarily good food, cooked with love and care,' and *The New York Times* says that 'the Irish soda bread and brown bread vie for star billing.'

The recipes, all Ballymaloe originals, are provided courtesy of Gill and Macmillan, publishers of **The Ballymaloe Cookbook.**

Tel: (021) 652531   Telex: 75208
Open: All year round
Prices: Dinner £20 Lunch £10.50

Leek, Potato and Cheese Pie

8 leeks
2 potatoes
3 tablespoons butter
Salt and pepper to taste
2 cups cheese sauce
½ clove crushed garlic
2 tablespoons grated cheese

Wash leeks and cut into rounds ½ inch thick. Peel and cut up potatoes to match the leeks. Melt butter in casserole dish. Toss vegetables in it and season them. Cover with a butter wrapper and a heavy lid and bake slowly until soft. Make a cheese sauce, adding a little crushed garlic to it. Mix the sauce with the vegetables and top with more grated cheese. It can be left like this until required. Cook at 375 degrees until heated through and brown on top. Serves six to eight.

French Peasant Soup

1 cup streaky bacon
½ cup onions
1 cup potatoes
½ cup cabbage
1 cup peeled, chopped tomatoes
½ cup stock
1 clove garlic
Salt and pepper to taste
½ teaspoon sugar

Dice vegetables and bacon neatly before measuring. Cook bacon until the fat runs. Add potatoes, onions and crushed garlic. Sweat for 10 minutes. Add cabbage and tomatoes seasoned well with salt, pepper and sugar. Cover with stock and boil until the cabbage is soft. Taste and adjust the seasoning. Serves five.

Lobster with Fresh Herbs and Cream

For each person:
1 cup lobster meat
2 teaspoons finely chopped
   shallot
½ cup dry white wine
½ cup lobster cooking water
¼ lb. sliced button mushrooms
Butter
Roux
1 teaspoon lemon juice
1 cup cream
1 teaspoon thyme leaves
1 teaspoon chopped parsley
2 teaspoons Hollandaise or
   Bearnaise sauce

Sauté mushrooms in butter for about a minute. Add lemon juice. Set aside. Toss semi-cooked lobster meat in foaming butter. Remove and then cook shallot in the same pan. After approximately 2 minutes add the white wine and reduce by half. Now add lobster cooking water and boil down again. Pull the pan aside and thicken with roux. Boil and stir. Remove from the heat again, add mushrooms and blend in cream. Boil up sauce for the last time. Taste for seasoning and stir in the herbs and Hollandaise or Bearnaise sauce. Stir in lobster meat. Fill back into heated shells and brown the top under a grill. If you add ½ cup grated cheese to the sauce and sprinkle more on the top you can call this dish Lobster Mornay. Serves one.

Cahernane Hotel
Killarney
County Kerry

The stunning Cahernane Hotel was once the private residence of the Earl of Pembroke. Erected on the Pembroke estate in 1877, this majestic building is surrounded by parklands and meadows against a backdrop of Killarney's lakes and mountains. While preserving an old-world atmosphere, the hotel offers modern amenities and exquisite food to its diners. Chef Edward Hayes supervises every aspect of food preparation for the hotel's two restaurants. The following recipes, favourites among Cahernane's guests, are his own creations.

Tel: (064) 31895   Telex: 73823
Open: Easter-Christmas
Prices: Dinner £22 (7-9pm)

Marinated Atlantic Salmon

12 ounces fresh salmon fillet
1 teaspoon sea salt
1 teaspoon red peppercorns
Juice of two limes
Several fresh coriander leaves

Skin salmon and trim dark meat and discard. With a salt mill sprinkle sea salt onto a plate. Slice salmon very thinly vertically and arrange neatly on salted plate. Sprinkle more sea salt on salmon and add red peppercorns. Just before serving squeeze lime juice over salmon and garnish with fresh coriander leaves. Serves four.

Gaelic Steak Flambé

2 lbs. beef tenderloin, trimmed
½ teaspoon dry mustard
4 ounces button mushrooms
2 shallots
2 ounces butter
1 clove garlic, crushed
2 tablespoons chives
4 ounces cream
1 jigger Irish whiskey
Salt and pepper to taste

Batten out tenderloins to ¼ inch thick. Dust with mustard. Slice mushrooms and finely chop shallots. Heat butter in copper pan. Add steak and seal both sides. Remove. Keep warm. Add shallots and mushrooms, garlic and chives. Sweat for 1 minute and add cream. Reduce sauce until thick. Add steaks. Heat tip of pan. Add whiskey and flame. Serves four.

Strawberry Rosette with Pineapple Cream

1 small pineapple
5 ounces whipping cream
1 jigger Irish Mist liqueur
8 ounces large strawberries
2 fresh mint leaves
Icing sugar

Remove skin and hard core from pineapple. Dice finely and add to stiffly whipped cream. Add Irish Mist liqueur. Arrange in centre of plate in a mound of sliced strawberries lengthwise with tips pointed outwards on top of pineapple. Tops with whipped cream. Decorate with mint leaves. Sprinkle all over with icing sugar. Serves four.

Ballynahinch Castle Hotel
Connemara
County Galway

Ballynahinch Castle, set in the heart of Connemara, is steeped in a wealth of tradition dating back to the sixteenth century. Many flamboyant figures from Irish history have owned this castle over the last 400 years, including Grace O'Malley, the infamous pirate queen whose portrait hangs over the fireplace in the hotel bar. Ballynahinch means 'household of the island,' referring to the castle's island location on the Ballynahinch River. Over the centuries the hotel has seen its share of lavish parties and opulent guests, and in 1834 the great Irish writer Maria Edgeworth said that the food was 'worthy of the greatest gourmet.' That statement still applies today.

Tel: (095) 31006   Telex: 50809
Open: All year round
Prices: Dinner £15-19 (7.30-9pm) Lunch £10 (1-2pm)

Irish Cream Soup

¼ lb. onion
¼ lb. leek
¼ lb. celery
¼ lb. mushroom stalks
2 ounces margarine or butter
2 ounces flour
5 cups chicken stock
1 ounce cream
¼ lb. pale Irish Cheddar cheese

Sweat off vegetables in melted butter without colour. Mix in flour. Cook over a gentle heat to a sandy texture without colour. Remove from heat. Cool slightly. Gradually mix in hot stock and cream. Stir to boil. Simmer 30 to 40 minutes. Skim if necessary. Pass through a sieve or strainer. Return to heat and reboil. Correct seasoning. Before serving put some small cubes of cheese in and leave to melt.

Mussels Chablis

10 pints mussels
1 bay leaf
1 sprig parsley
1 shallot
6 black peppercorns
1 pint dry white wine
5 ounces heavy cream
2 egg yolks
2 tablespoons chopped parsley
Black pepper to taste
Lemon juice

Clean the mussels thoroughly, discarding any with broken or open shells. Scrape away all grit and remove the beards. Put the mussels in a large, heavy-based saucepan with the bay leaf, parsley and the finely chopped and peeled shallot. Add the peppercorns. Pour the wine over all. Cover the pan with a lid and cook the mussels over a high heat until the shells open. As the shells open remove the mussels from the pan. Throw away the empty shells (top halves) and place the mussels in their half shells in a warmed casserole. Cover then with a clean cloth to prevent them from drying out and to keep warm. Strain the cooking liquid through muslin. Mix the cream and egg yolks together in a bowl and blend in a few tablespoons of the mussel liquid. Add to the remaining liquid, together with the chopped parsley. Season to taste with the freshly ground pepper and lemon juice. Reheat the liquid without boiling until it has thickened slightly. Serve the mussels in individual deep soup plates, with the sauce poured over them. Set a finger bowl with a slice of lemon by each plate. Offer plenty of crusted bread and provide a spare bowl or plate for the empty mussel shells. Serves four to six.

Hotel Ard-na-Sidhe
Killarney
County Kerry

One of three luxurious hotels run by Killarney Hotels, Ltd., Hotel Ard-na-Sidhe is a well-preserved Victorian mansion located in one of the most beautiful areas of Ireland. The hotel, the name of which is Irish for 'the height of the fairies,' is a cosy escape spot for those looking for a quiet holiday and good food. The tastefully furnished interior features beautiful antiques, period furniture and an open fireplace. Located on the edge of Canagh Lake, guests like to fish and boat to work up an appetite for the restaurant's delicious cuisine.

Tel. (064) 31900   Telex: 73913
Open: May-September
Prices: Dinner £18 (7-9pm)

Veal Steak

5 ounces veal steak
Thin slice marinated or smoked
  salmon
2 king prawns
1 teaspoon butter
1 portion leaf spinach
2 shallots, chopped
1 teaspoon cream
Salt and pepper to taste
1 clove garlic

Mustard Sauce
1 tablespoon mustard
1 tablespoon sour cream
½ teaspoon dried dill tips
½ teaspoon chopped shallots
Salt and black peppercorns to
  taste

Mix sauce together until blended and set aside. Cut veal steak butterfly style and batten lightly. Spread meat with mustard sauce. Add slice of marinated salmon, king prawns and small piece of butter. Close the two flaps and fasten with a skewer. Fry at low heat with butter. Clean and wash spinach leaves. Sauté in butter with shallots and cook for 2 to 3 minutes with a dash of cream. Season with salt, pepper and garlic. Serve on top of leaf spinach garnished with diced Ogen melon and choron sauce. Choron sauce is tomato-flavoured bearnaise sauce. Serves two.

Brown Trout Fried with Oatmeal

1 large trout
1 lemon
Salt and pepper to taste
½ cup flour
1 egg
½ cup oatmeal flakes
2 tablespoons butter
Lemon and parsley garnish

Clean trout and season with lemon, salt and pepper. Dip in flour and then eggwash and press lightly in oatmeal flakes. Put in hot pan with melted butter and bake at 225 degrees for 10 minutes. Garnish with lemon and parsley. Pour the butter over the trout. Serve with salad and potatoes. Serves two.

Celtic Mews Restaurant
Dublin

From its handsome decor to its intimate atmosphere to its fine food, the Celtic Mews is thoroughly Irish. Run by Joe and James Gray and family since 1973, the restaurant features every detail of good service and fine food. Head chef Willie Woods uses only the best local produce. Woods and head waiter Tony Conlon have been with the Celtic Mews from its beginning, and both contribute to the family feeling their guests enjoy.

Tel: (0001) 760796
Open: All year round
Prices: Dinner £20-25 (6.30-11.30pm) Lunch functions

Veal Killarney

2 lb. loin of veal
1 ounce flour
2 eggs, separated
1¼ cup milk
½ cup breadcrumbs
1 lb. mushrooms
2 ounces butter
2 tablespoons tomato purée
4 slices of cooked ham
1 tablespoon chopped parsley
A little fond de veau

Cut the veal into four portions. Remove the eye from each and reserve the trimmings to make the fond de veau. To do this boil the trimmings in a little water and allow it to reduce. Batten out the veal and dust it lightly in flour. Beat the egg yolks with the milk and dip the veal in it. Coat with breadcrumbs. Fry the veal in a little oil until golden brown and cooked through. Place on a serving dish and keep hot. Peel and slice the mushrooms and cook in melted butter. Meanwhile, reheat the fond de veau. Add the tomato purée and cook for a few minutes. Place a slice of the cooked ham over each of the veal portions. Add the cooked mushrooms and pour over a little of the butter. Surround the meat with the fond de veau. Sprinkle with chopped parsley and serve. Serves four.

Fillets of Sole Dublin Bay

3 large fresh sole, approximately
16 ounces
2 ounces margarine
2 ounces flour
1 pint milk
6 cups fish stock
Salt and pepper to taste
2 eggs
Mashed potatoes
1 lb. fresh prawns, peeled
2 tablespoons Parmesan cheese

Skin and fillet the sole. Place the fillets in a flat pan. Cover with a little cold water and poach gently until cooked. Remove from the pan and place on a dry cloth. Cook the liquid a little more and allow to reduce by about half. Make a bechamel sauce by melting the margarine in a saucepan. Add flour and mix thoroughly until the mixture is dry and comes away easily from the side of the pan. Reduce the heat and add the milk and fish stock a little at a time, stirring all the while to avoid curdling. Cook for a few minutes until the sauce is of a light and smooth consistency, then season. Separate the eggs and add the yolks to the mashed potatoes with a little seasoning. Using either a large dish or four separate dishes, pipe an oval of the potato mixture around the side. Into the centre place the sole fillets, allowing three per person. Divide the prawns between the four portions and place on top of the sole. Spoon the sauce over the fish. Sprinkle with Parmesan cheese. Then place under the grill for a few minutes until lightly browned and serve. Serves four.

Lovetts
Douglas
Cork City

Lovetts is a charming, country cottage-style restaurant on Churchyard Lane in Douglas. Entirely family-operated, the restaurant prides itself on the high percentage of guests who return time and again to enjoy their traditional and gourmet cuisine. The specialty of the house is fresh fish simply cooked with light sauces, but Lovetts also has a fine reputation for its tasty desserts and fresh-baked breads.

Tel: (021) 294909/362204
Open: All year round
Prices: Dinner £16-18 Lunch £10

Plaice in a Green Jacket

Per person:
1 fillet of plaice, skin removed
A few large lettuce leaves, lightly
  blanched
Knob of butter
1 cup fish stock

Lay out the leaves on board. Place fish on top and completely cover by folding over lettuce. Place on a greased baking tray. Put a knob of butter on top. Add a little fish stock and cover with buttered paper. Bake at 400 degrees for 12 to 15 minutes.

Bailey's Iced Soufflé

6 egg yolks
1 whole egg
5 ounces sugar
½ glass white wine
2½ cups cream
1 cup Bailey's Irish Cream
  liqueur

Beat egg yolks, egg, sugar and wine over a pot of hot water until very light and creamy. Beat cream until slightly stiff. Fold cream into egg mixture. Fold in Bailey's and freeze for 1 hour. Remove and stir well with a metal spoon to prevent Bailey's from sinking. Freeze again. Serves four.

Chocolate Carrageen Mousse with Irish Coffee Sauce

Mousse
1 cup dried carrageen moss
3¾ cups milk
3 tablespoons cocoa
2 tablespoons sugar
½ teaspoon vanilla essence

Soak the carrageen for 10 minutes in warm water. Remove and rinse. Place moss in saucepan with milk. Bring to a boil and simmer gently. Add cocoa which has been blended with a little milk, vanilla and sugar. Simmer for an additional 20 minutes. Strain into a mixing bowl. Capture any jelly.

Irish Coffee Sauce
1 cup sugar
⅓ cup water
1 cup coffee
3 tablespoons Irish whiskey

Dissolve one cup of sugar in ⅓ cup of water over heat until it forms a caramel. Remove from heat. Pour in one cup of coffee and continue cooking until the caramel dissolves. Do not stir. Cool and add Irish whiskey. Pour over mousse. Serves four.

Dunraven Arms Hotel
Adare
County Limerick

The beautiful village of Adare, which dates from the time of the Norman Conquest, owes its captivating appearance to the third Earl of Dunraven, who designed and laid out the village in the nineteenth century. At the heart of Adare is the Dunraven Arms, where four generations of the Dunraven family have looked after visitors. Under the guidance of head chef Tadg Moylan, the hotel's Maigue Restaurant has received the Bord Failte Award of Excellence. In the summer months patrons are entertained by traditional Irish fiddlers, singers and storytellers, making the Dunraven a popular gathering spot for both locals and tourists.

Tel: (061) 86209   Telex: 70202
Open: All year round
Prices: Dinner £16 (7.30-9pm) Lunch £7 (12.30-2pm)

Brown Scones

1 lb. white flour
1 lb. brown flour
4 teaspoons baking powder
Pinch of salt
8 ounces margarine
4 tablespoons honey
4 eggs
1¼ cup buttermilk

Mix together flours, baking powder and salt. Rub in margarine and honey. Make a well in the centre and add eggs and some of the buttermilk. Knead lightly to a smooth dough. Place on a flour board. Roll out and cut as desired. Place onto a well greased tray and bake at 350 degrees for approximately 20 minutes.

Roast Duckling with Black Cherry Sauce

1 duck

Sauce
1 small can of black cherries
3 fluid ounces thick brown sauce
  (demiglace)
2 tablespoons of red currant jelly
2 tablespoons corn syrup
½ glass of port

Roast the duckling for 1½ hours at 350 degrees. Halve and debone. Coat with the black cherry sauce. To make sauce, drain the juice from the cherries. Add the rest of the ingredients to the juice. Bring to a boil. Reduce to a nice coating consistency. Remove the stones from the cherries. Warm the cherries in the sauce. Serves four.

Coquilles St. Jacques Dunraven Arms

2 medium scallops
½ glass brandy
½ glass dry white wine
½ finely diced shallot
2 medium-sliced mushrooms
1 finely diced deseeded tomato
1 teaspoon chopped parsley
1 teaspoon chopped chives
5 ounces cream
Salt and pepper to taste

Quickly sauté the scallops in a hot pan. Flame with the brandy. Add the white wine. Bring to a boil. Remove the scallops. Add the mushrooms, tomato, parsley and chives. Reduce this by half. Add the cream and reduce to a light, flowing consistency. Add the scallops. Correct the seasoning and serve in the scallop shells. Serves four.

Devilled Cucumber and Tomato Soup

1 gallon chicken stock
5 ounces tomato purée
2 medium cucumbers
4 fluid ounces malt vinegar
2 teaspoons Worcestershire
  sauce
Juice of two lemons
2 sprigs chopped dill
1¼ cup sour cream
Salt and pepper to taste

Add the stock to the tomato purée. Finely dice the cucumber. Add the cucumber and the rest of the ingredients to the soup. Season to taste. Chill for 2 hours. Serves ten.

Bill Parrish

The Vintage Restaurant
Kinsale
County Cork

Every October, the town of Kinsale hosts a five-day international food festival that attracts gourmet food lovers from all over Europe. The Vintage figures prominently in these festivities, which have earned Kinsale the reptuation as the 'gourmet centre of Ireland.' Master Chef Michael Riese, formerly head chef at the Four Seasons Hotel in his native Hamburg, uses only organically grown vegetables, free-range fowl and rabbits, eggs from free-range chickens and seafood caught just offshore. Cosy, romantic, The Vintage features an open fire in the dining room, 200 year-old beams and the original masts from ships that sailed into Kinsale Harbour over a century ago.

Tel: (021) 772502
Open: mid March-mid January
Prices: Dinner £15 (7-9pm)

Pork Fillets in Roquefort Sauce

8 medallions of pork fillet,
weighing 2¾ ounces
Salt and ground black pepper to
taste
¾ ounce olive oil
2 cloves garlic, unpeeled
1 sprig rosemary
1½ ounces young carrots, cut
into sticks
1½ ounces celery, cut into sticks
2 ounces mange-tout

Sauce
½ ounce butter
¼ ounce finely chopped shallot
1½ ounces dry white wine
1 ounce cider
4 ounces brown veal stock
2 ounces heavy cream
1½ ounces Roquefort cheese,
cut in small pieces
Salt and ground pepper to taste

Season the well-trimmed medallions of pork with salt and pepper. Heat the olive oil and butter. Add the pork. Put in the garlic cloves and sprig of rosemary. Sauté the pork on both sides over a moderate heat. Do not overcook them. Remove the meat and keep warm. Discard the fat. Sauce: heat the butter in the pan. Add the finely chopped shallot and sweat. Add wine and cider. Reduce. Add veal stock and reduce to half its original volume. Strain. Boil up and add the cream. Put in the cheese and season with salt and pepper. Cook the carrots, celery and mange-tout separately until just crisp, then add to the sauce. Arrange the sauce on a warm plate with the medallions of pork on top. Serve immediately. Walnuts, peeled and sautéed in butter may be added to this dish to enrich it. Serves four.

Kiwi Sorbet with Champagne

1¾ lbs. kiwi fruit
4 ounces water
7 ounces champagne
5 ounces sugar
¼ ounce vanilla sugar
Juice of ¼ lemon
1 tablespoon Pernod

Peel the well-ripened kiwis and liquidize them. Boil the water, champagne, sugars and add to the purée of kiwi fruit. Cover and allow to cool. Finish with lemon juice and Pernod. Pass the mixture through a fine sieve. Freeze. Serves four. (Note: The kiwi is also known as a Chinese gooseberry.)

The Fisherman Restaurant
Annalong
County Down

The Fisherman is owned and run by the Bowens, former owners of a restaurant in New York City's Greenwich Village who fell in love with the village of Annalong eight years ago, pulled up stakes and moved there. Chef Bill likes the idea of being able to get fresh fish off the boats of Kilkeel each morning. People come from as far as Dublin and Belfast to sample his famous fish dishes, but the meat and chicken entrées are equally appealing.

Tel: (03967) 68733
Open: All year round
Prices: Dinner £10 (6-9pm)

Prawns with Garlic and Basil

2 ounces butter
2 cloves garlic, finely chopped
2 lbs. prawns, shelled
1 tablespoon parsley,
  finely chopped
1 tablespoon basil, finely chopped
Juice of ½ lemon
2 tablespoons chopped scallions
Salt and freshly ground pepper
  to taste
1 teaspoon paprika

Heat butter and garlic in a heavy skillet. Add prawns, parsley, basil, lemon juice and scallions. Turn prawns, basting them in the sauce until they turn white, about 5 minutes. Add salt and pepper and cook for 1 additional minute. Sprinkle on paprika and serve on a bed of seasoned rice. Serves four.

Seasoned Rice

1 cup uncooked rice
½ teaspoon turmeric
A pinch of mixed herbs
1 chicken bouillon cube

Cook rice as usual, rinse and strain. Return rice to pan. Cover with water and add turmeric, herbs, chicken stock cube and bring to a boil. Strain and serve.

Poached Turbot with Prawn Sauce

4 turbot fillets
Court bouillon
8 ounces dry white wine
8 ounces water
1 slice of lemon
1 bay leaf
1 sprig of parsley
6 peppercorns
1 small stalk of celery
½ teaspoon salt

Simmer for about 20 minutes and strain. Poach turbot in court bouillon until cooked for about 10 minutes. Place on serving platter and spoon on prawn sauce. Serves four.

Prawn Sauce
1 pint milk
1 slice onion
8 peppercorns
1 bay leaf
1 small piece celery
Blade of mace
2 ounces butter
3 tablespoons of flour
Pinch of thyme
8 anchovies, finely chopped
1 lb. prawns
1 tablespoon finely
  chopped parsley
Salt and freshly ground pepper
¼ teaspoon freshly
  grated nutmeg

Heat milk, onion, peppercorns, bay leaf, celery and mace together until it simmers. Remove from heat. Cover and stand for 20 minutes. Strain. Make a roux in a heavy saucepan with butter, flour, thyme and anchovies. Add milk stock and bring to a boil, stirring frequently. Add prawns, parsley, salt, pepper and nutmeg. Simmer until prawns are cooked, about 15 minutes.

Tinakilly House Hotel
Rathnew
County Wicklow

Constructed in the 1870s for Captain Robert Halpin, the man who laid the first telegraph cable linking Europe and North America, Tinakilly House has been fully restored by current owners William and Bee Power, who have kept the original Victorian furnishings. A constantly burning log fire in the lofty main hall completes the decor of this perfect blend of Victorian splendour and 1980s comfort. The hotel's three dining rooms have won international acclaim for their blend of country-house cooking and nouvelle cuisine prepared by head chef Christian Proust.

Tel: (0404) 69274   Telex: 80412
Open: All year round
Prices: Dinner £21.50 Lunch £12

Steamed Breast of Chicken on a Raspberry Flavored Yogurt Dressing

2 chicken breasts
1 ounce diced onion
1 ounce diced leek
1 ounce diced carrot
1 ounce diced celery
2 ounces fresh tarragon
1 cup chicken stock
1 cup white wine
Salt and pepper to taste
8 ounces natural yogurt
3 tablespoons raspberry vinegar

Place the chicken breasts in a small roasting tray and sprinkle diced vegetables and tarragon on top. Mix the chicken stock, white wine, salt and pepper. Pour into the dish. Cover with the lid and lightly poach for 10 minutes after boiling. Remove from heat. Leave to cool. Meanwhile, mix the yogurt and vinegar in a bowl. Cover the entire surface of a plate with the dressing. Carve the chicken breast very thinly and arrange on the centre of the plate in a fan shape, using half breast per portion. Garnish with fresh tarragon leaves and an orange segment. Serves four.

Brace of Quail with Lemon Balm

Small bunch of fresh lemon balm
4 ounces butter
8 quail, prepared and cleaned
4 sprigs of lemon balm
Julienne of radish
1 cup demiglace

Blend the lemon balm and the butter until creamy. Stuff the quail with balm butter. Seal on a hot pan and bake in the oven at 300 degrees for 15 minutes. Place the quail in the centre of the plate, two per portion, and garnish with a sprig of lemon balm and radish. Pour the hot demiglace around the birds. Note: Two tablespoons Irish Mist liqueur gives an excellent flavour to the sauce. Serves four.

Bee's Brown Bread

13 ounces coarse ground
   wholemeal
7 ounces self-rising flour
1 teaspoon salt
1 teaspoon baking soda
1 tablespoon brown sugar
5 ounces buttermilk

Preheat oven to 400 degrees. Mix all ingredients together with a knife and mix in the buttermilk. Combine. Do not knead. Scoop into a greased two-pint casserole dish. Cover with a lid and bake in the middle of the oven for approximately 1 hour.

Doyle's Seafood Bar
Dingle
County Kerry

The top good food guides have bestowed the highest awards time and again on Doyle's Seafood Bar in Dingle. Stella and John Doyle run every aspect of this informal restaurant. The menu features fresh seafood, chosen daily from the fish landed by Dingle boats. All shellfish are kept alive in a *vivier* tank and cooked to order. Although the produce is local, the restaurant has a strong French/Italian influence with a healthy mix of Irish traditional. Stella Doyle spends time abroad every year working under the tutelage of Europe's great chefs, while John likes to travel to foreign vineyards, purchasing wine for Doyle's impressive cellar.

Tel: (066) 51174
Open: mid March-mid November
Prices: Dinner £14 (6-9pm)

Cockle and Mussel Soup

40 whole mussels
20 whole cockles
2½ cups white wine
2½ cups milk
6 cups crab stock
6 cups lobster stock
1¼ cups roux
2½ cups milk
2½ cups cream
Pepper to taste

Cook the mussels and cockles in white wine until opened. Remove from shell and chop. Add crab and lobster stock. Add roux and chopped mussels and cockles to sauce and bring to boil. Leave to simmer on low heat for 20 minutes. Then stir in milk and cream. Season with pepper. Serves six.

Irish Onion Soup

4 ounces butter
4 sliced onions
4 ounces flour
1 bottle white wine
1½ quarts chicken stock
Salt and pepper to taste
1¼ cups milk
1¼ cups cream

Melt butter and add shredded onions. Cook until tender. Add flour, then wine. Let it bubble for a minute or two. Add chicken stock and salt and pepper and let it cook for about 30 minutes. Add milk and cream and cook for 10 minutes more. Serves eight.

The Step House
Borris
County Carlow

Located between the foothills of Mt. Leinster and the banks of the River Barrow is the small village of Borris, where the late-Georgian Step House, fully restored and furnished in its original period style, caters to appreciative locals and tourists. To please their discerning clientele, the proprietors of The Step House use only the freshest ingredients. Dinner is served in the warm, inviting atmosphere of candlelight and an open log fire.

Tel: (0503) 73209
Open: April-November
Prices: Dinner £18 (6.30-10pm)

Step House Fish Soup

2 tablespoons oil
1 large onion, sliced
1 leek, trimmed, split and sliced
1 clove garlic
1 stick celery, sliced
1 lb. tomatoes, peeled, seeded and chopped, or 1 large can tomatoes
1¼ cup fish stock (more stock may be added if necessary)
2 tablespoons parsley
Salt and pepper to taste
Bourquet garni
½ lb. prawns, peeled
1 lb. monkfish
1 smoked kipper fillet
1 dozen mussels, cleaned
Tomato purée to taste, optional

Heat oil in large pan. Sauté onion, leek, garlic and celery for 5 minutes without colouring. Add tomatoes (if canned tomatoes are used add juice), stock, 1 tablespoon parsley, salt, pepper and bouquet garni. Bring to a boil and simmer for 20 minutes. Add prawns, monkfish and kipper and cook for 5 to 8 minutes. Add mussels in their shells and cook until they open. Remove bouquet garni, add 1 tablespoon parsley. Adjust seasoning. Use tomato purée if desired. Serves six.

Ris d'Agneau Tante Marie

1 lb. sweetbreads
Slice of lemon
¼ teaspoon salt
1¼ cup stock, chicken or veal
1-2 tablespoons oil
1 ounce butter
4 ounces button onions
1 clove garlic
4 tablespoons sherry
5 ounces white wine
Bouquet garni
4-5 bread croutes
4 ounces button mushrooms
1 tablespoon tomato purée
Kneaded butter
2 ounces cream

Soak the sweetbreads in salted water for 1 to 2 hours. Then put into a pan, cover with fresh cold water and add lemon and a little salt. Bring to a boil. Drain, rinse and press between two plates until quite cold. Put something on top of the plate. A weight makes it possible to see the fat more clearly for trimming. Trim away any gristle and return to the pan. Barely cover with stock and simmer 10 to 15 minutes. Drain well and dry the sweetbreads. Reserve 8 ounces of the stock. Blanch button onions in cold water, covered, 2 to 3 minutes. Heat the oil. Add butter, onions and garlic. Cook 2 to 3 minutes. Add the sweetbreads and allow to brown. Dust with the flour. Flame with the sherry. Add the wine, reserved stock and bouquet garni. Season and simmer for 35 minutes. Meanwhile fry the croutes in butter, lift out and arrange on the serving dish. Sauté the mushrooms briskly in the same pan, leaving them whole. Set aside. Take up the sweetbreads, slice to ¼ " thick if necessary and arrange on the croutes. Add the tomato purée to the liquid in pan and thicken with a little kneaded butter. Reboil, adjust the seasoning, add the cream and mushrooms. Boil for 1 to 2 minutes, then spoon over the sweetbreads. To make croutes, take slices of bread, trim crusts and cut in half. Fry in butter until golden brown. Do not drain. Arrange on serving plate. Serves six.

Dunadry Inn
Dunadry
County Antrim

On the site of an old mill town dating from the eighteenth century, the Dunadry Inn overlooks the old mill stream. A perfect blend of old-time charm and modern comfort, the inn has a constantly changing atmosphere—the hustle and bustle of a lunchtime buffet gives way to a quiet, traditional afternoon tea followed by evening elegance, including their regular Saturday night dinner dance. But every dish, whether for a banquet or a romantic dinner for two, is prepared with individual care and expertise.

Tel. (08494) 32474   Telex: 747245
Open: All year round
Prices: Dinner £15 (7.30-9.45pm) Lunch £7.50
  (12-2.30pm)

Chicken Tandragee

For each person:
1 breast of chicken
1 slice avocado pear
2 teaspoons cream cheese
1 beaten egg
2 ounces breadcrumbs

Make a pocket in each chicken breast and stuff with blended avocado and cream cheese. Dip in beaten egg and coat with breadcrumbs. Deep-fat-fry for approximately 10 minutes.

Antrim Shore Lobster

1 lobster (live)
1 ounce butter
1 tablespoon white wine
1 tablespoon Irish Mist liqueur

Sauce
2 ounces butter
2 ounces flour
1 pint fish stock
1 cup white wine

Combine ingredients and simmer on low heat for 15 minutes. Cook lobster in boiling water. Remove from shell and dice the flesh. Sauté in butter and white wine and flame with liqueur. Make up sauce and add to meat. Return to washed lobster shell and serve. Serves one.

Apple Dunadry

4 apples
2 tablespoons sweet mince
2 teaspoons Bushmills whiskey
2 teaspoons brown sugar

Sauce
1¼ cups milk
Cornstarch to thicken
2 drops vanilla essence
1 teaspoon Bushmills whiskey

Peel and core apples and fill centres with sweet mince, whiskey and sugar mix. Bake at 350 degrees for 30 minutes or until tender. Boil milk and thicken with corn starch. Add vanilla and whiskey and pour over apples. Serves four.

Cashel Palace Hotel
Cashel
County Tipperary

Ancient and historic Cashel was for seven centuries the seat of the kings of Munster. It was also here that St. Patrick first used the shamrock as a religious symbol of the Trinity, giving Ireland its most famous trademark. Cashel Palace, an elegant Palladian mansion built in 1730, served as a bishop's residence for 230 years. Now a luxury hotel with elegant rooms, magnificent gardens and gourmet dining, the Palace's motto is *Tranquility in an Age of Change,* perfectly illustrated by the Bishop's Walk, a peaceful, pleasant walkway leading from the hotel to the famous Rock of Cashel, which provides a superb romantic vista.

Tel: (062) 61411   Telex: 70638
Open: All year round
Prices: Dinner £18-26 (7-9.30pm) Lunch £10 (1-2pm)

Baked Pear en Papilotte

2 tablespoons Cointreau
1 orange zest and juice
1 teaspoon honey
1 teaspoon sugar
2 ounces stock syrup
1 ripe pear

Place Cointreau, orange juice and zest, honey, sugar and syrup in copper pan. Bring to a boil for 2 minutes. Peel pear. Remove pulp. Cut in half, then cut in fan shape lengthwise. Place pear on aluminum foil. Cover with Cointreau syrup. Seal aluminum foil. Bake at 375 degrees for 5 minutes. Serve with orange zest garnish. Serves one.

Lobster Kathleen

1 good sized lobster, 1½-2 lbs.
Sea salt and whole white pepper
  to taste
1 ounce butter
3 shallots, chopped fine
1¼ cups fish stock
2½ cups white wine
1¼ cups cream
6 scallions, chopped fine
1 jigger Irish whiskey
Fresh fennel

Cut lobster in half lengthwise. Crack claws. Season with sea salt and pepper. Cover with butter. Place under the grill for 10 to 15 minutes. Sauté shallots in a little butter. Add fish stock and wine. Reduce by half. Add cream and reduce by half again. Remove lobster from grill. Arrange on oval plate. Add scallions and Irish whiskey to sauce. Pour sauce over lobster. Garnish with fennel. Serves two.

Irish Blue Flambé

3 ounces Cashel blue cheese
2½ cups olive oil
4 ounces breadcrumbs
1 leaf iceberg lettuce
1 leaf Chinese cabbage
Bunch of watercress and chervil
1 tomato, julienned
½ leek, chopped
3 scallions, chopped
3 strawberries, julienned
3 blackberries, julienned
Salt and pepper to taste
1 tablespoon butter
1 jigger brandy

Marinate cheese in olive oil for 2 hours. Drain and reserve olive oil. Toss in breadcrumbs. Mix lettuce, cabbage, herbs, tomato, leeks, scallions and fruit together. Season with salt and pepper and sauté in butter. Heat olive oil to smoke-point. Fry off cheese on all sides until crispy. Flambé with brandy. Serve with sautéed salad. Garnish with watercress. Serves one.

King Sitric, The Fish Restaurant
Howth
County Dublin

With dishes as delightful to the eye as they are to the palate, this quietly elegant restaurant has won many international food awards. Named after King Sitric III, a Norse king of Dublin during the eleventh century, the restaurant offers a magnificent view of Howth Harbour, one of the largest fishing ports in Ireland. Chef/proprietor Aidan McManus takes full advantage of the port, offering fresh lobster, salmon, brill, crab and other fine sea dishes to his customers. All fish dishes are accompanied by the restaurant's famous traditional Irish brown bread.

Tel: (0001) 325235/326729
Open: All year round
Prices: Dinner £16-26 (6.30-11pm) Lunch £11 (12.30-2.30pm)

King Sitric Brown Bread

1¼ lbs. wheatenmeal
4 ounces plain flour
1 teaspoon baking soda
1 teaspoon salt
2 teaspoons sugar
3 cups buttermilk
1 ounce melted butter

Mix the flours, soda, salt and sugar. Add the milk and knead until thoroughly mixed (a very wet mixture). Add the butter. Put into a hot casserole dish and cover with a lid, into a preheated oven and bake at 400 degrees for one hour. Remove and cover with a damp cloth. Makes a 3 lb. loaf.

Avocado à la King

1 small green pepper, diced
4 ounces mushrooms, sliced
1 tablespoon olive oil
2 egg yolks
2 large ripe avocados
1¼ cups heavy cream
½ lemon
Salt and pepper to taste

Cook the peppers and mushrooms in a little olive oil over a low heat. Season. Add the cream, bring to a boil and reduce by one half (or until it is nearly at sauce consistency). Meanwhile, halve the avocados, discard the seeds and remove the flesh, using a teaspoon. Dice. Add to the sauce and bring to a boil. Add the lemon juice and remove from heat. Stir in two slightly beaten egg yolks and place in the skins in avocado dishes and glaze under the grill for 5 minutes. Serves four.

Escalope of Salmon with Honey and Lemon

2-3 slices of salmon cut from a
  fillet (about 6 ounces)
1 tablespoon honey
1 teaspoon lemon juice
1 teaspoon butter per portion

Cook the salmon for 1 minute on each side in a non-stick skillet with the honey, lemon juice and butter. Season. Plate the fish and strain the sauce over it. Serves two.

Marlfield House Hotel
Gorey
County Wexford

Once the principal residence in Ireland of the Earl of Courtown, Marlfield House is now a stunning tribute to the elegance the building knew in the nineteenth century, when the earl entertained aristocratic families from all over Britain and Ireland. The present owners, Mary and Ray Bowe, have restored the sweeping curved staircase, the drawing room's crystal chandelier and the exquisitely appointed guestrooms, refurbished in original Regency-period decor. Herbs and vegetables for the hotel restaurant are grown out back, and a well-stocked wine cellar complements the gourmet food that has won Marlfield House many awards.

Tel. (055) 21124
Open: All year round
Prices Dinner £18-25 (7.30-9.30pm) Lunch £13 (1-2.30pm)

Chocolate and Hazelnut Mousse

4 leaves gelatin
2 eggs, separated
2 ounces granulated sugar
1¼ cups milk
2 ounces chocolate couveture
1¼ cups cream
2 ounces chopped hazelnuts

Soak the gelatin in cold water. Cream the egg yolks and sugar in a bowl until almost white. Bring the milk to a boil and dissolve the chocolate in it. Whisk in the milk, mixing well. Return to a low heat and stir constantly with a wooden spoon until the mixture coats the back of the spoon. The mixture must not boil. Remove from the heat. Add the gelatin. Stir until dissolved. Place in a clean bowl and leave to cool, stirring occasionally until almost setting point. Fold in lightly beaten cream, then the stiffly beaten egg whites. Finally, add the chopped hazelnuts. Serves four.

Roast Stuffed Leg of Lamb
with Caramel and Mint Sauce

Stuffing

1 small leg of lamb with the aitch-bone and knuckle removed
1 medium onion
2 tablespoons mixed herbs
2 ounces butter
½ loaf white breadcrumbs
Salt and pepper to taste
¼ bag of mixed nuts

Lamb Stock

½ lb. carrots
1 large onion
3 stalks celery
1 leek
1 clove garlic
½ cup tomato purée
3 pints cold water

Caramel and Mint Sauce

2 ounces granulated sugar
1 tablespoon chopped mint

Sweat off onions and fresh herbs in butter. Then add the breadcrumbs and season. Add chopped mixed nuts afterwards. Place in leg of lamb.

Brown carrots, onion, celery, leek and garlic with the knuckle and aitchbone. Add tomato purée and cold water and bring to a boil. Skim when necessary. Simmer up to 2 hours, reducing by half.

Place sugar in a saucepan and caramelize. Add reduced lamb stock and simmer for 10 minutes. Add the chopped mint.

Place the stuffed leg of lamb in a roasting tray and season before cooking. Cook in a preheated oven for 50 minutes to 1 hour at 425 degrees. As the knuckle bone is removed the lamb will cook more quickly. Pink lamb is much more flavoursome. Serves eight.

Chocolate Whiskey Cake

1 lb. butter
1 lb. chocolate, half dark and half light
4 eggs
6 ounces sugar
1 jigger whiskey
4 ounces walnuts
4 ounces cherries
1½ lbs. good quality digestive biscuits (or graham crackers)

Melt butter and chocolate together over gentle heat. Beat eggs and sugar until creamy. Add whiskey. Chop walnuts and cherries and break biscuits. Put biscuits, walnuts and cherries in a dish. Add egg mixture to chocolate and ladle onto biscuits. Refrigerate for 2 hours. Serves six.

Egan's House
Glasnevin
County Dublin

John and Betty Egan love to spoil visitors to their large, family-run guesthouse, Egan's of Iona Park. The Egan tradition includes a cheery atmosphere and hearty food. All of the cooking is done by Betty, for whom cooking comes as natural as breathing. For many of her creations, she does not even have a recipe, knowing instinctively what combination of ingredients is right.

Tel: (0001) 303611
Open: January-mid December
Prices: Dinner £15 (7-9.30pm)

Bailey's Irish Cream Cheesecake

½ lb. Philadelphia cream cheese
1 glass of Bailey's Irish Cream
  (or to taste)
2 ounces granulated sugar
1 teaspoon lemon juice
1 teaspoon coffee
Digestive biscuits
  (or graham crackers)
1½-2 ounces butter
2½ cups cream
1 packet unflavoured gelatin

Cream the cheese, Bailey's Irish Cream, sugar, lemon juice and coffee (dissolve the coffee in a little hot water first). Crush the biscuits (the amount depends on how thick you want the base). Bind with melted butter. Press firmly and evenly in a 12″ cheesecake pan and leave in refrigerator until needed. Add lightly whipped cream to creamed cheese. Add dissolved gelatin. Whip lightly until creamy. Pour over the base and put in the refrigerator until set.

Homemade Brown Bread

1 lb. white flour
½ lb. brown flour
1 teaspoon baking soda
1 teaspoon salt
2½ cups buttermilk

Mix all dry ingredients well together. Make well in centre and add buttermilk, a little at a time, and mix well. Add more buttermilk until you have a smooth consistency. Turn onto floured board. Lightly knead and then turn onto floured baking pan. Bake at 200 degrees for 10 minutes and then at 175 degrees until done, about 45 minutes.

Sea View Hotel
Ballylickey
County Cork

The palatial Sea View Hotel is owned and managed by Kathleen O'Sullivan, who has converted this stunning country house into a hotel and restaurant. Ideally suited to tourists of the West Cork and Kerry regions, the restaurant is recommended by Ashley Courtenay, Egon and Michelin guides, and is the recipient of the AA Red Star and Rosette Awards. After a day of golfing on nearby courses, angling, pony trekking or exploring the hotel's beautiful grounds, a sumptuous dinner at the Sea View is just the thing for a hearty appetite.

Tel: (027) 50462
Open: mid March-mid October
Prices: Dinner £16 (7.30-9pm) Lunch £9 (1-2pm)

Fillets of Sole à L'Orange

4 fillets of sole from 1 lb. fish
Juice of one large orange
1 ounce butter
¾ teaspoon Tabasco sauce
Salt and pepper to taste
Fresh orange segments to
  garnish

Poach fillets slowly in orange juice for 8 to 10 minutes in warm oven, 250 degrees. Remove and keep warm. Add butter and Tabasco sauce to the juice. Season. Swill the pan until butter melts. Reduce slightly. Strain round fillets on warm plates and place segments on the side. Serves four.

Fillets of Sole Vermouth

Per person:
2 mushrooms
1 tablespoon oil
4 fillets of sole from a 1 lb. fish
1 sherry glass of vermouth
1 sherry glass of cream
1 teaspoon butter
Salt and pepper to taste

Sauté the sliced mushrooms in oil and place fillets on top. Add vermouth and bring to a boil. Cover and place in warm oven, 250 degrees, for 8 to 10 minutes. Remove fillets from pan and keep warm on the side. Add cream and butter. Check seasoning. Pour sauce on warm plates and fillets on top. Serves one.

index

Pear, baked en Papilotte, 93
Plaice in a green jacket, 78
Plaice stuffed with mussels, 37
Pork, casserole of, 20
Pork fillets in Roquefort sauce, 82
Pork steak, medallions in apricot sauce, 64
Potato bread, 26
Potato cakes, 6
Potatoes, Gaby's creamed, 55
Potato soup, Bunny's, 22
Prawn bisque, 46
Prawn cocktail, Dublin Bay, 12
Prawns Provençale, 43
Prawns, sautéed in tomato and garlic, 63
Prawns with garlic and basil, 83

Quail with lemon balm, 86
Quennels of turbot in prawns, 50
Quiche, Aillwee, 8
Quiche Ashbourne style, 63

Red mullet with cognac, 59
Ris d'Agneau, 90

Sachertorte, Austrian, 40
Salmon, baked, 21
Salmon, dressed whole, 28
Salmon escalope, 96
Salmon, fresh Mayo, 18

Salmon, marinated Atlantic, 70
Scones, brown, 79
Sea bass, grilled with leek and soya butter, 34
Sea bass with seaweed, 60
Seafood, money bags of, 50
Seafood mosaic, 56
Seasoned rice, 84
Sea trout with seafood stuffing, 64
Smoked salmon noodles, 40
Soda bread, Auntie's Irish, 30
Sole à l'orange, 100
Sole, delice of, 54
Sole Dublin Bay, 76
Sole vermouth, 100
Steak, fillets in cream sauce, 64
Steak Haven, 44
Strawberry rosette, 70

Tripe with onions, 32
Trout, baked stuffed, 24
Trout with spinach, 36
Turbot, poached with prawn sauce, 84
Turbot Poche Bonne Femme, 62

Veal escalope, 48
Veal Killarney, 75
Veal, Midas, 52
Veal steak, 74

Whiskey mousse, 46